When you need to choose between better and best, God knows which is which—don't hesitate to ask him.

PRESENTED TO

_____

PRESENTED BY

_____

DATE

_____

Contentment is an invisible line. It's the line between "I need" and "I want."

LIVING SIMPLY

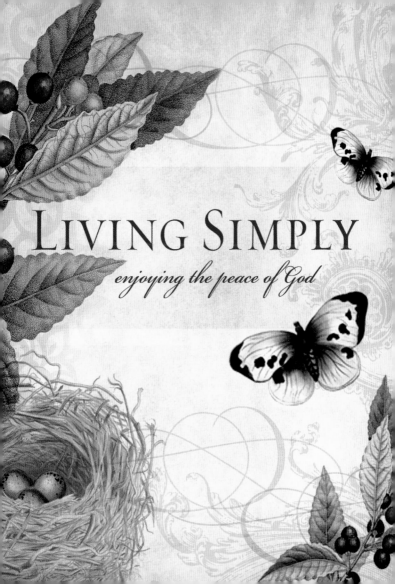

LIVING SIMPLY

enjoying the peace of God

Living Simply

Copyright © 2012 by Renewing Minds Press
Oklahoma City, Oklahoma 73179

Printed in China.

13 14 15/HK/ 4 3 2 1

One step at a time, and that well placed,
We reach the grandest height;
One stroke at a time, earth's hidden stores
Will slowly come to light;
One seed at a time, and the forest grows;
One drop at a time, and the river flows
Into the boundless sea.

Author Unknown

I have learned the secret of being content in any
and every situation, whether well fed or hungry,
whether living in plenty or want. I can do everything through him who gives me strength.
Philippians 4:12–13 NIV

TABLE OF CONTENTS

INTRODUCTION

Life is complex, and time seems to spin by faster each day. You're tired of feeling squeezed by demands and pressured to go even faster. And you wonder, *Is it possible to live a simpler, more restful life?*

Absolutely—and you can start right now.

Here, forty meditations offer insights and suggestions to help you discover God's gift of inner peace and soul-soothing serenity. So put your feet up. Lean back. Embrace the simple life you dream about.

The simple life is an unencumbered life,
emotionally as well as physically.

UNPACK YOUR BAGS

"Forget the former things; do not dwell on the past.
See, I am doing a new thing!" says the Lord.

Isaiah 43:18–19 NIV

The simple life is an unencumbered life, emotionally as well as physically. Sometimes, however, the pain of the past just won't let go. Take a few childhood disappointments. Add some minor resentments, major regrets, and painful injustices. Before you know it, you're on your way to having a matched set of emotional baggage. It would be nice if getting rid of it were as easy as leaving it at God's doorstep, running the other direction, and never having to look at it again. But if you don't take time to unpack any emotional baggage you've acquired, you can end up carrying it around the rest of your life. Your mind will continue to replay unpleasant memories. Your body will be weighed down with anxiety, possibly resulting in stress-related illnesses. Your spirit will never fully experience the joy God has planned for you. That's because a heart filled with yesterday has no room to fully enjoy today.

The apostle Paul knew the importance of putting his past behind him. At one time, he was a powerful Jewish leader who persecuted and killed followers of Christ. Then he had a personal encounter with Jesus. His direction changed in an instant, though that didn't change his past. And yet the positive, life-changing biblical letters Paul later wrote, such as the letter to the Philippians, are filled with forgiveness and hope, not past regret. Paul unpacked the emotional baggage of the man he was to become the new man God created him to be.

Choosing to unpack emotional baggage is similar to cleaning out a suitcase after a trip. With emotional baggage, begin by throwing away trash (past resentments and bitterness) and taking steps to forgive those who've hurt you. With your personal dirty laundry (guilt or regret over things you've done or neglected to do), apologize or make necessary amends to those you've wronged. That includes apologizing to God and learning to forgive yourself.

Put everything you're holding on to in its proper place so you can focus on what lies ahead.

ONE FINAL THOUGHT

Taking time to unpack the emotional clutter of yesterday allows you to more fully enjoy God's irreplaceable gift of today.

Thoughts for Living Simply

One thing I do: Forgetting what is behind and straining toward
what is ahead, I press on toward the goal to win the prize for
which God has called me heavenward in Christ Jesus. All of us
who are mature should take such a
view of things.
Philippians 3:13–15 NIV

Reflect upon your present blessings, of which every man has plenty; not
on your past misfortunes, of which all men
have some.
Charles Dickens

Leave your troubles with the Lord, and he will defend you; he
never lets honest people be defeated.
Psalm 55:22 GNT

Trust the past to God's mercy, the present to God's love, and the future
to God's providence.
Saint Augustine of Hippo

Remember...

_____God can use your past as a wise teacher for your present and future.

_____Not a day goes by when God isn't doing a new thing in your life.

_____God is strong enough to carry your heaviest emotional baggage.

_____Take a lesson from Paul and choose joy over regret.

Simplify...

Make the first move to talk things out when relational problems arise.

Hand your problems to God every evening before you go to sleep.

Throw out any memorabilia that brings to mind negative situations.

Consult a counselor to help you unpack traumatic emotional baggage such as abuse or grief.

Forgiveness not only blesses the lives of those you forgive, but also lightens your own emotional load.

Don't let yesterday take up too much of today.
Will Rogers

TURN DOWN THE VOLUME

*Let us keep our silent sanctuaries for in them the
eternal perspectives are preserved.*

Etienne Senancour

Some noise is soothing—a gentle breeze rustling autumn
leaves, a tender lullaby, the voice of a friend. Too often, however, a cacophony of unwanted sounds clutters modern life—
pounding jackhammers, ringing cell phones, honking horns.
Excessive noise isn't healthy for you. Trying to mentally
tune out noise while you're completing tasks stresses your
body by making it work harder. Noise increases
your pulse rate and blood pressure, makes your
adrenaline surge, and depletes your energy.

Noise not only takes a toll on your mind
and body. It also takes a toll on your soul. A
mind that cannot quiet down will have trouble
hearing God's voice. Jesus often went off into
the wilderness to pray. He knew the value
of a quiet place away from the crowds,
and he tried to instill the importance
of these silent sanctuaries into the
lives of his followers. In Mark 6:31

16

(NIrV) Jesus said to his apostles, "Come with me by yourselves to a quiet place. You need to get some rest." So they left by boat for a quiet place.

If you have a park near your home or office, pray while taking a walk in it or spend time on a park bench reading the Bible as a great way to briefly retreat from clamor.

If you don't have the luxury of retreating to a more serene location, you can create a quiet place at home. It can be anywhere—the corner of your bedroom or den, a chair on the porch, or the bathtub. Where you have your quiet place doesn't matter so much as that you prepare it. Close the windows to shut off outside distractions. Turn off your cell phone, radio, and TV. Ask other members of your household not to disturb you for a set amount of time. Then tell God the concerns of your heart. Listen in silent expectation for his answers and words of encouragement. They may not always come right away. But the more comfortable you are with silence, the easier it is to hear God whisper.

ONE FINAL THOUGHT

Building silent sanctuaries into your life will not only benefit your body, but will also help you better understand the one who created it.

Thoughts for Living Simply

"Be still, and know that I am God."
Psalm 46:10 NIV

It is in silence that God is known, and through mysteries that he declares himself.
Robert Hugh Benson

I am content and at peace. As a child lies quietly in its mother's arms, so my heart is quiet within me.
Psalm 131:2 GNT

O Lord, the Scripture says, "there is a time for silence and a time for speech." Savior, teach me the silence of humility, the silence of wisdom, the silence of love, the silence of perfection, the silence that speaks without words, the silence of faith. Lord, teach me to silence my own heart that I may listen to the gentle movement of the Holy Spirit within me and sense the depths which are of God.
German Prayer

Remember...

_____Elijah did not hear God in the wind, the earthquake, or the fire, but in a still, small voice.

_____Jesus made time for silence and knew the value of a quiet retreat.

_____A quiet heart is attentive to and can hear God's gentlest whisper.

_____Silence is a gift that reduces stress and nurtures your spirit.

Simplify...

Run a quiet fan to dull background noise and help to improve your concentration.

Reflect during pauses in conversation instead of talking just to break the silence.

Cultivate quiet by establishing a set family break from TV and telephone calls. Retreat to a silent sanctuary at least ten minutes each day.

Break the habit of listening to music just for background noise.

One who can keep a thought-filled and active silence for more than two minutes can hold anyone for two hours.
Adela Rogers Saint Johns

SETTING TRAPS FOR PACK RATS

The more possessions, the more worry.
Hillel

A small child fills his pocket with seashells as he toddles along the beach. A young boy counts his allowance—one more time— to make sure he has enough for that next coveted pack of baseball cards. A teenage girl places yet another stuffed bear on the already overcrowded comforter on her bunk bed. The desire to acquire is a battle that begins in childhood and continues into old age.

While you may gain a certain joy in hunting for yet another painting of Elvis on black velvet or a junker car you feel compelled to bring back to life, you will pay a price. And that price is not just what disappears from your wallet. You pay the price in the time you spend shopping for, cleaning, repairing, and eventually disposing of the treasures you choose to fill your home.

Jesus may have been called many things during his time here on earth, but he was never called a pack rat. Though the last three years of his life were spent traveling, the Gospels don't mention Jesus picking up even one souvenir along the way. He encouraged his disciples to travel light, leaving their extra staffs and tunics and even money behind. Granted, Jesus and his disciples depended on the generosity of those in the villages they visited to meet their physical needs. First and foremost, however, they chose to live a simple life, possessing only what they needed for their mission.

Living a simple life isn't synonymous with taking a vow of poverty. But making prayerful purchases and being resolute in getting rid of things you no longer need will help you go a long way toward cleaning up the clutter in your life. If something's broken, fix it or get rid of it. When it comes to paper, file it or toss it. Learn to appreciate the beauty of something without having to own it. Most importantly, keep the unique mission God has given you in this life clearly in mind. Then, let your home be a reflection of that purpose.

ONE FINAL THOUGHT

With God's help, your heart should determine how much your hands will hold.

Thoughts for Living Simply

Jesus said, "Watch out and guard yourselves from every kind of greed; because your true life is not made up of the things you own, no matter how rich you may be."
Luke 12:15 GNT

Remember that when you leave this earth, you can take with you nothing that you have received—only what you have given: a full heart enriched by honest service, love, sacrifice and courage.
Saint Francis of Assisi

Jesus said, "Store up for yourselves treasures in heaven, where moth and rust do not destroy, and where thieves do not break in and steal. For where your treasure is, there your heart will be also."
Matthew 6:20–21 NIV

You will never be satisfied with impermanent, passing things, for you were not created to find your rest in them.
Thomas á Kempis

Remember...

_____The riches God speaks highly of are those that can be stored in the heart.

_____People are eternal, but things break, get lost, and wear out.

_____Being intentional in your spending leaves you with more money to use as God leads.

_____Heaven's gates aren't wide enough for you to bring along a moving van.

Simplify...

Run a quiet fan to dull background. Make a list before you go shopping, and then stick to it.

Refuse to collect anything except friends. When you go on vacation, say no to souvenirs.

Give excess possessions away to charity.

Choose somewhere other than the mall to spend your free time.

There is nothing wrong with us possessing riches.
The wrong comes when riches possess us.
Billy Graham

PRESCRIPTION FOR PEAK PERFORMANCE

Do you not know that your body is a temple of the Holy Spirit, who is in you, whom you have received from God? You are not your own; you were bought at a price. Therefore honor God with your body.

1 Corinthians 6:19–20 NIV

Life would be simpler if your body was low maintenance. Think of how much free time you would have if
you didn't need that time-consuming eight hours of sleep.
Balanced diet? You could eat chocolate bars morning,
noon, and night—or nothing at all if your workload
outweighed the need for a lunch break. And if
you were in some unfortunate accident, you
could just slap on an adhesive bandage and be
back in business.

The physical body is a fragile gift that
needs daily maintenance. Ignoring the care
your body needs may save you time—at
least at first—but it won't simplify your
life. A body that has been deprived of
exercise, adequate sleep, a nutritious diet,
and consistent dental care tends to break
down more often. The few minutes you
originally saved by not flossing could
result in hours in a dentist's chair facing

gum surgery. Most maintenance activities are a small price to pay, both in time and money, compared to the serious consequences that can result from putting your health in last place on your to-do list.

You only get one physical body in this life, and it is a gift. God gave you another gift as well—the privilege of free will. That free will allows you to choose how to maintain your body and soul. How you care for the life he's given you is a reflection of how much you appreciate the sacrifice it took for him to offer it to you.

But your body is an incredibly complex creation, and there are countless tips on how to keep it healthy. Trying to follow them all could end up complicating your life. So stick to the basics. Get a good night's sleep. Eat a balanced diet. Watch your weight. Schedule annual medical and dental checkups. Exercise several times a week. Do what you can. Then put your physical health into God's loving hands. He can take care of the details that are out of your control.

ONE FINAL THOUGHT

Your physical body is a priceless gift—how you take care of it is your thank-you note to God.

Thoughts for Living Simply

Jesus said, ...Whatever you do, whether you eat or drink,
do it all for God's glory.
1 Corinthians 10:31 GNT

*Look to your health; and if you have it, praise God, and value it next
to a good conscience; for health is the second blessing that we mortals are
capable of; a blessing that money cannot buy.*
Izaak Walton

Jesus said, "Store up for yourselves treasures in heaven, Train
yourself to be godly. For physical training is
of some value, but godliness has value for all things, holding
promise for both the present life and the
life to come.
1 Timothy 4:7–8 NIV

He who enjoys good health is rich, though he knows it not.
Italian Proverb

Remember...

_____Taking care of your body in a way that honors God is one way of worshiping him.

_____The blessing of a good night's sleep lasts long after your alarm goes off.

_____Much of Jesus' ministry was spent healing, showing his care for the human body.

_____Taking care of your health contributes to a better quality of life.

Simplify...

Supplement your diet with a daily multivitamin.

Go to bed every night at the same time to help establish more restful sleep patterns.

Make fast food the exception when eating out.

Take the stairs instead of the elevator whenever possible.

Exercise with a friend for encouragement to remain consistent.

If you don't take care of your body, where are you going to live?
Author Unknown

SATISFACTION GUARANTEED

Keep your lives free from the love of money and be content with what
you have, because God has said, "Never will I leave you; never will I
forsake you."

Hebrews 13:5 NIV

If you have a sweet tooth, you're probably familiar with the power of freshly baked chocolate chip cookies. The scent of melting chocolate mixed with butter and vanilla fills the entire house. When the timer finally goes off, you probably disregard the recommended cooling time and eat a cookie straight out of the oven. Momentarily you're content. But the cookie was so good you reach for another, then another. If you continue eating in hopes of reliving that one moment of satisfaction, the cookies may stop tasting good altogether. You no longer feel content. You feel stuffed—even discontent. You can have too much of a good thing. You know the feeling.

Contentment is an invisible line. It's the line between "I need" and "I want." Whether it's a chocolate chip cookie, a better job, or a bigger house, identifying that line begins with a heart check. A heart that is filled with gratitude for God's daily blessings is less likely to long for mere "wants" which do not have the ability to provide deep, lasting satisfaction. James 1:17 (NIV) says that "every good and perfect gift is from above." These are the kind of gifts that are longed for by the heart, not the eyes. And these God-given treasures nurture both thankfulness and contentment.

Relaxing in the comfort of "enough" has the power to simplify your life. It will help you reduce the number of possessions that clutter your home. It will release you from striving financially and emotionally after things you don't need but wish you had. It will lessen the desire to compare your lifestyle with those around you. It will also help you gain a greater appreciation for what you already have.

A simple life is a contented life, and a contented life begins with a thankful heart. Spend time each and every day thanking God for all he's given you, and be content.

ONE FINAL THOUGHT

Giving thanks blesses God and makes contentment a reality in your life .

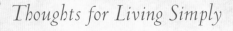

Thoughts for Living Simply

I have learned the secret of being content in any and every situation, whether well fed or hungry, whether living in plenty or want. I can do everything through him who gives me strength.
Philippians 4:12–13 NIV

Contentment is a pearl of great price, and whoever procures it at the expense of ten thousand desires makes a wise and a happy purchase.
John Balguy

Godliness is actually a means of great gain when accompanied by contentment. For we brought nothing into the world, so we cannot take anything out of it either. If we have food and covering, with these we shall be content.
1 Timothy 6:6–8 NASB

The heart is rich when it is content, and it is always content when its desires are fixed on God. Nothing can bring greater happiness than doing God's will for the love of God.
Migel Febres Cordero-Munzo

Remember...

_____God alone can satisfy every longing in your heart.

_____Jesus was content with the life his Father set before him.

_____Saying grace before meals helps you be content with what's on your plate.

_____Whatever God in his wisdom, grace, and love provides is enough.

Simplify...

Shop to fill physical needs; pray to fill emotional ones.

Learn to distinguish the invisible line between "I need" and "I want."

Write God a thank-you note in your mind each night before going to sleep.

Throw away the department store circulars from the Sunday paper without looking at them.

Consistently pray for help in differentiating between your needs and wants.

The word "content" comes from a Latin root meaning "to hold together." When we are content, our lives hold together.
R. Benjamin Garrison

31

THE POTENTIAL OF THIS MOMENT

No longer forward nor behind I look in hope and fear; but grateful, take the good I find, the best of now and here.
John Greenleaf Whitter

Whenever you possibly can, do good to those who need it. Never tell your neighbors to wait until tomorrow if you can help them now.
Proverbs 3:27–28 GNT

Lord, let me know my end, and what is the measure of my days; let me know how fleeting my life is.
Psalm 39:4 NRSV

Let us not grow weary in doing what is right, for we will reap at harvest time, if we do not give up. So then, whenever we have the opportunity, let us work for the good of all, and especially for those of the family of faith.
Galatians 6:9–10 NRSV

One step at a time, and that well placed,
We reach the grandest height;
One stroke at a time, earth's hidden stores
Will slowly come to light;
One seed at a time, and the forest grows;
One drop at a time, and the river flows
Into the boundless sea.

Author Unknown

A MATTER OF BALANCE

Things which matter most should never be at the mercy of things which matter least.

Johann Wolfgang von Goethe

Modern life is often referred to as a juggling act. You wake up each morning with a number of balls at your fingertips, such as your career, family, health, civic duties, household responsibilities, friendships, and your relationship with God. The more balls you're responsible for, the more complex the task of juggling them seems. In addition to learning how to juggle, you also need to learn how to walk the tightrope.

While responsibilities can be juggled, priorities must be balanced. As any tightrope walker will agree, finding the proper balance takes practice. Before you start moving, you have to carefully find your center. As you move forward, you have to constantly readjust to maintain balance. You lean to the right, only to need to move quickly to the left.

Balancing your priorities will help simplify your life. Accomplishing this balance takes similar focus, adjustment, and readjustment to that of a walking a tightrope. When you're faced with the choices of spending some much needed, quality time with your spouse, working overtime to meet a deadline, or attending a church committee meeting you've previously committed yourself to, the perfect balance can be hard to find.

You begin balancing the same way a tightrope walker does, by finding your center before moving forward. The only unchanging center is God. The deeper you grow in relationship with him, the more balanced your life and priorities become. In tightrope walking and in life, it is also easier to maintain your equilibrium if you're using a bar to balance. Mark 12:30–31 is the heart of perfect balance—love God with all your heart, soul, mind, and strength and love your neighbor as yourself. Through Bible reading, prayer, and seeking to follow where God leads in your life, you can move forward with confidence, unwavering in your purpose and priorities.

ONE FINAL THOUGHT

Priorities balanced on the firm foundation of God's Word are less likely to topple under pressure.

Thoughts for Living Simply

Jesus said, "Put God's kingdom first. Do what he
wants you to do."
Matthew 6:33 NIRV

*The older I get the more wisdom I find in the ancient rule of taking
first things first. A process which often reduces the most complex human problem to a manageable proportion.*
Dwight Eisenhower

Be imitators of God, therefore, as dearly loved children and
live a life of love, just as Christ loved us and gave himself up
for us as a fragrant offering and sacrifice to God.
Ephesians 5:1–2 NIV

*All things proceed from God, who is at once the center and the circum-
ference from which all existing lines proceed and at which all end up.*
Juana Inés de la Cruz

Remember...

_____The Bible is an accurate scale on which to weigh every priority you're trying to balance in life.

_____One of Jesus' highest priorities was making sure that you would be able to spend eternity with him.

_____When you feel out of balance, the wisdom you need to set things right is only a prayer away.

_____In God's eyes, loving people is a high priority.

Simplify...

Write a personal purpose statement for your life to gain insight into your priorities.

Memorize Mark 12:30–31 and weigh decisions in light of its commands.

Pray that God will help you make the right choices to simplify your life.

Simplify your schedule by eliminating commitments that are low priorities in your life.

Set aside a special time this week to work on the high priority relationships in your life.

Look over last week's schedule and ask what you would change if you lived it according to God's priorities.

Erwin W. Lutzer

CHANGING CHANNELS

*My friends, fill your minds with those things that are good and that deserve
praise: things that are true, noble, right, pure, lovely, and honorable.*

Philippians 4:8 GNT

Throughout the centuries people have been drawn to
storytellers, minstrels, and entertainers of every kind. God
designed the human mind to be creative and to crave both
learning and laughter. Your mind functions like your physical body. When you fill your body with healthy, wholesome
food, it performs at its peak. When you fill your mind with
wholesome thoughts, including those inspired by positive
entertainment, it has the food it needs to mature
and grow in a healthy way. Just as taking care of
your body simplifies your life, so also does taking
care of your mind.

That's why being intentional in what you
choose to watch on TV really does matter. A
few decades ago, options were simple. You
had a couple of fuzzy, black-and-white
channels to choose from. Today you
can choose between basic cable,
digital, or satellite dish, all
broadcasting twenty-four hours

a day. Program topics vary dramatically, and your choices reflect your mind-set or point of view.

When it comes to television, simplifying your life begins with streamlining your choices to support and encourage the way of thinking that you desire. Consider the programs you watch every week. Which ones fall within God's guidelines of good taste? Which ones are true, noble, right, pure, lovely, and honorable? Be your own censor. Turn on the TV only when there is something worth watching on. If you're in need of a little entertainment and the only program you can find to watch is visual junk food, expand your entertainment possibilities by eliminating cable. Pick up a good book. Write a letter. Play a card game or board game with friends or family. Take a nice long bath. Call a friend. Sing along with your favorite CD. Make a list of things you'd like to do if you had some free time.

Read your Bible instead of the television lineup, and fill your mind with life-changing truths. Reserve television viewing for programs that will enhance your relaxed life.

ONE FINAL THOUGHT

Give your mind a workout every time you sit down to watch TV— exercise your good judgment.

Thoughts for Living Simply

O Lord, you have searched me and known me. You know when I sit down and when I rise up; you discern my thoughts from far away.

Psalm 139:1–2 NRSV

The TV is my shepherd, my spiritual life shall want. It makes me to sit down and do nothing for the cause of Christ. It demandeth my spare time . . . Surely comedy and commercials shall follow me all the days of my life, and I will dwell in spiritual poverty forever.

Author Unknown

Do not conform any longer to the pattern of this world, but be transformed by the renewing of your mind. Then you will be able to test and approve what God's will is—his good, pleasing and perfect will.

Romans 12:2 NIV

Let each man think himself an act of God, his mind a thought, his life a breath of God.

Philip James Bailey

Remember...

_____God's guidance is just as available when choosing channels as when choosing careers.

_____You never watch TV alone; Jesus is always by your side.

_____Loving God with your whole mind includes the parts of your mind that watch TV.

_____Positive entertainment encourages positive thoughts.

Simplify...

Choose to either read the newspaper or watch the evening news rather than do both.

Make a family schedule for TV viewing and stick to it.

Decide what you're going to watch before you pick up the remote.

Limit your options by limiting the number of channels you are able to receive.

Fast from TV for one week and see how many ways you

Give me, kind heaven, a private station,
a mind serene for contemplation.
John Gay

Just Say No—When God Says So

I have always walked in your way and have never strayed from it.

Psalm 17:5 GNT

The word boundaries brings to mind pictures of confinement and limitation—fences, rules, border checks, out of bounds, or keep out! signs. Yet boundaries are also safeguards to freedom. The same boundary markers that keep you from wandering off course allow you to walk unhindered to your destination. That's why setting appropriate boundaries for yourself helps simplify your life. Boundaries can protect you from wasting your energy on detours.

Think of yourself as a gallon of paint. You choose the color. Say you were created to cover about 200 square feet. However, the wall looming ahead of you is 250 square feet. When asked if you're up to the job (and assuming for this scenario that paint can speak), you say yes. You don't want to look like a quitter in front of the rest of the latex. Perhaps the challenge sounds kind of intrigu-

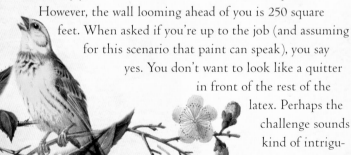

ing. Or maybe you're just too shy to say no. Whatever the reason, you know the outcome. You have to spread yourself too thin, and the result is an inferior paint job. Your true color isn't evident.

Study the life of Jesus to learn how to set better boundaries. Jesus drew limits to minister effectively to countless people. He said yes to personal time for prayer, solitude, celebration, and relationships. He also made time for unscheduled interruptions, such as the chance to hug a child or heal a leper. Jesus' last words were, "It is finished" (John 19:30 NIV). He had finished what he had to do in the time the Father had given him.

Jesus said no. He didn't heal everyone, and he had only twelve disciples. Saying no to what you don't need to do gives you the freedom to say yes to what God has created you to do. Through prayer and the study of his Word, God can help you set boundaries that will provide you with both the focus and the breathing room a simple life requires.

One Final Thought

No is a positive word when it's used to set boundaries that keep you from spreading yourself too thin, allowing your true colors to shine.

Lord, I am always with you; you hold me by my right hand.
You guide me with your counsel.
Psalm 73:23–24 NIV

Lord, may I be directed what to do and what to leave undone.
Elizabeth Fry

[The Macedonian churches]
gave themselves first to the Lord and then to us in
keeping with God's will.
2 Corinthians 8:5 NIV

*History has a sense, a meaning, a direction; it goes somewhere, and
necessarily in a good direction—the Messiah.*
Elie Wiesel

Remember...

_____Jesus could have re-
mained on earth healing
people, but he said no to a
good opportunity in order to
say yes to a better one.

_____Doing a job with excel-
lence is only possible when
you're operating within the
physical, mental, and emotional
limits God has set for you.

_____When you need to
choose between better and best,
God knows which is which—
don't hesitate to ask him.

_____You are unique in design,
so your personal boundaries
will also be unique.

Simplify...

*Resist outside pressure or
persuasion to turn your no into
a yes.*

*Say "Let me think about it" in
response to any on-the-spot commitment you're asked to make.*

*Allow yourself to turn down
an opportunity without feeling
obligated to explain why.*

*Get counsel from those closest to
you, including God, before making any important commitment.*

*Accept a no answer from others
with the same grace you'd like
for them to extend to you.*

*It is almost as presumptuous to think you can do nothing
as to think you can do everything.*
Phillips Brooks

45

KEEPING YOURSELF IN THE BLACK

There is nothing that makes men rich and strong but that which they carry inside of them. True wealth is of the heart, not of the hand.

John Milton

Think about this question: Would more money make your life simpler? How much would it take for you to comfortably meet your expenses? If your answer is "just a little bit more," you're not alone. The problem is, if you're spending even a little bit beyond your present income, that little bit can eventually add up to a lot. Making more money won't guarantee you a simpler life—only living within your means can do that.

Living within your means requires that you live in the real world. Using credit allows you to live in a world of illusion. It encourages you to play the part of someone whose budget is not your own. You can dress, eat, drive, travel, and play the part of a person of wealth without a cent in your pocket. However, playing king or queen for most people can only be a temporary role. Tomorrow always comes, and with it comes complications.

The way to get the most out of tomorrow is to appreciate your limits and find contentment within your means today. A budget allows you to reconcile your outgo to your income and to live within the limits. A budget also encourages imagination, creativity, and possibilities within your means, which in turn nurtures heart contentment.

Maintaining a budget, seeking wise financial counsel, refusing to live in the fantasy world of credit, and keeping yourself in the black are all positive steps toward a simple life. The more you treasure riches that cannot be held in your hand, the less of a hold living beyond your means will have on your heart, and your heart is where the success of any plan ultimately lies. Heart contentment can help you avoid any overspending problem.

ONE FINAL THOUGHT

*Simplify your future—live within your means today,
so you won't be paying for yesterday tomorrow.*

 *Thoughts for Living Simply*

Honor the Lord with your wealth, with the firstfruits of all
your crops; then your barns will be filled to overflowing, and
your vats will brim over with new wine.
Proverbs 3:9–10 NIV

Wealth, after all, is a relative thing, since he that has little and wants
less is richer than he that has much and wants more.
Charles Caleb Colton

Give everyone what you owe him: If you owe taxes, pay taxes;
if revenue, then revenue; if respect, then respect; if honor, then
honor. Let no debt remain outstanding, except the continuing
debt to love one another.
Romans 13:7–8 NIV

In this world it is not what we take up, but what we give up that makes
us rich.
Henry Ward Beecher

Remember...

_____Your present income is both a gift and an opportunity— a gift from God and an opportunity to enjoy contentment.

_____The more you are in debt, the more difficult it is to live within your means.

_____The riches that bring the most contentment are those that spring from the heart.

_____Money is a tool to be understood and managed.

Simplify...

Resist outside pressure. Keep only one credit card, for emergency use only, and pay off the balance every month.

When you have to replace a car, buy used. Pay cash, if possible.

Put cash for entertainment and dining out into an envelope once a month. Then, spend only what's available.

Track your spending with the help of budgeting software.

Learn more about Christian credit counseling from Dave Ramsey http://www.daveramsey.com/ or Crown Financial Ministries http://www.crown.org/.

When your outgo exceeds your income, your upkeep is your downfall.
Phillip H. Barnhart

ORGANIZING BY THE NUMBERS

Let all things be done properly and in an orderly manner.

1 Corinthians 14:40 NASB

The possibilities of what you can do with one twenty-four-hour period are endless. On one hand, that's an exciting prospect. On the other, all of those options can lead to opportunity overload. Accomplishing what you have to do, and at the same time incorporating what you'd like to do in your day, is a complex task. What you need is a sieve, a tool that can help you sift away what is inconsequential, while retaining what is most important. A simple written list is that kind of a tool. It can help you organize and prioritize, which will simplify your life.

Even God used a list. On a mountaintop, God told Moses that the Israelites should love and honor him with their lives. Then God summarized how in a list of ten things. He put the list in priority order, beginning with how he should be treated. He continued on with how family should be treated and ended with how other people should be treated. God gave Moses two stone tables, carved with his own hand, containing these commandments. God wrote them down so the Israelites wouldn't forget.

While your daily to-do list doesn't need to be carved in stone, taking the time to write one will simplify your life by helping you become more successful in accomplishing what really matters. God's priceless gift of time always honors him when it is well spent.

Take a few minutes each morning to order your day. Ask for God's help in prioritizing tasks, organizing them by what must be done, what should be done, and what you'd like to get done. Pencil in some extra time for the unexpected. Review your list from the previous day. If your list was unfinished, ask God to help you reevaluate what you can accomplish in a single day.

ONE FINAL THOUGHT

When you take time each morning to organize your day, you'll find you have more time to spend on what's most important.

Thoughts for Living Simply

A prudent man gives thought to his steps.
Proverbs 14:15 NIV

Good order is the foundation of all good things.
Edmund Burke

Be careful how you live. Don't live like ignorant people,
but like wise people. Make good use of
every opportunity you have.
Ephesians 5:15–16 GNT

He who every morning plans the transactions of the day and follows
out that plan carries a thread that will guide him through the laby-
rinth of the most busy life . . . If the disposal of time is surrendered
merely to the chance of incident, chaos will soon reign.
Victor Hugo

Remember...

_____You have twenty-four hours every day to accomplish what you want.

_____From the Ten Commandments to genealogies to blueprints for God's Temple, the Bible uses lists to organize tasks and information.

_____When honoring God is at the top of your to-do list, the rest of your day falls more easily into order.

_____God is the author of organization, which is evident in everything he's created from DNA to the grandest galaxy.

Simplify...

Keep your to-do list in your purse or wallet, so you can refer to it during the day.

Keep a running grocery list on the refrigerator, adding to it anytime you use up an item.

Maintain a running list of calls to be returned. Schedule one time daily to return them.

Break large tasks down by making a list of smaller steps you need to do to accomplish them.

Be realistic about what you can accomplish in a day and eliminate those things that you don't need to do.

Routine is God's way of saving us between our times of inspiration.
Eileen Altenburg

THE SIMPLE PRACTICE OF PRAYER

Aspire to God with short but frequent outpourings of the heart; admire His bounty; invoke His aid; cast yourself in spirit at the foot of His cross; adore His goodness; treat with Him for your salvation; give Him your whole soul a thousand times a day.

Saint Francis de Sales

Pray in the Spirit on all occasions with all kinds of prayers and requests.

Ephesians 6:18 NIV

Jesus said, "When you pray, go into your room. Close the door and pray to your Father, who can't be seen. He will reward you. Your Father sees what is done secretly. When you pray, do not keep talking on and on the way ungodly people do. They think they will be heard because they talk a lot. Do not be like them. Your Father knows what you need even before you ask him."

Matthew 6:6–8 NIRV

Arise, cry out in the night, as the watches of the night begin; pour out your heart like water in the presence of the Lord.

Lamentations 2:19 NIV

For the beauty of the earth,
For the beauty of the skies,
For the love which from our birth
Over and around us lies:
Christ, our God, to thee we raise
This our sacrifice of praise.

For the beauty of each hour
Of the day and of the night,
Hill and vale and tree and flower,
Sun and moon and stars of light:
Christ, our God, to thee we raise
This our sacrifice of praise.

Folliot Sandford Pierpoint

TIME OUT FOR TIME OFF

God blessed the seventh day and made it holy, because on it he rested from all the work of creating that he had done.

Genesis 2:3 NIV

Relaxation . . . the word itself almost seems as if it could lower your blood pressure. It brings to mind featherbeds, sunny shores, and lazy afternoons spent without an agenda. It's tempting to believe that the simplest life would be one that revolves around this type of schedule, devoid of anything remotely related to commitment, busyness, or work. But in its truest form, a simple life is a godly life that balances purposeful labor with times of rest.

Maintaining this balance enables you to do the purposeful work God has given you to do and be your best. By contrast, physical and mental exhaustion can do more than make you cranky. Exhaustion can lower your resistance to fight off illness and increase your chances of making mistakes, both big and small, which will complicate your life. Rest and relaxation, however, give you both a physical and a spiritual boost. Though God has no need for physical rest, even he took a day off after creating the universe. He balanced his labor with a time of rest, enjoying what he had accomplished.

Follow God's example. When you work, work hard, throwing yourself wholeheartedly into whatever task is at hand. When you rest, leave work behind and let yourself really relax. That means refraining from doing paperwork in front of the television or checking in with the office during your family vacation. Instead, kick back with both your mind and body and celebrate what you've accomplished.

You can better balance your simple life by making rest and relaxation a regular part of your schedule. Begin with a good night's sleep. When life gets busy, being fully rested yields more long-term benefits than setting the alarm earlier to try and get more done. Take breaks during your workday. Whether you're working at a computer or shoveling concrete, take a five-minute break every hour. Get up and stretch. Close your eyes, breathe deeply, and relax.

ONE FINAL THOUGHT

Relaxation is the godly counterpoint to diligent labor needed to balance a simple life.

Thoughts for Living Simply

I am worn out, O Lord; have pity on me! Give me strength; I
am completely exhausted.
Psalm 6:2 GNT

*Recreation is not the highest kind of enjoyment, but in its time and place
it is quite as proper as prayer.*
Saint Irenaeus

There is still a Sabbath rest for God's people. God rested from
his work. Those who enjoy God's rest also rest from their work.
So let us make every effort to enjoy that rest.
Hebrews 4:9–11 NIRV

*O Lord, support us all day long, until the shadows lengthen and the
evening comes, and the busy world is hushed, and the fever of life is over,
and our work is done. Then in thy mercy grant us a safe lodging, and a
holy rest, and peace at the last.*
John Henry Cardinal Newman

Remember...

_____Rest and relaxation are good gifts given by a God who knows exactly what you need.

_____A simple life is a godly life.

_____Being fully rested yields longer lasting benefits than cutting sleep short to get more done.

_____God's presence is an ever-present destination for relaxation.

Simplify...

Relax and reflect by listening to a CD with your eyes closed.

Leave the cell phone behind when you take a break, whether for an hour or a week.

Make a list of things that relax you. Work your way down the list during your free time.

Treat yourself to a mini vacation by taking a walk during your lunch break.

Cut caffeine and television right before bedtime, since they can both be stimulants and disturb your rest.

God rest you merry.
Dinah Maria Mulock Craik

The Ultimate Pick-Me-Up

The clever do all things intelligently.

Proverbs 13:16

No matter where you live—in the suburbs or the city, on an estate or in a double-wide—there's one thing every home has in common. Homes need to be kept up. Eating, sleeping, wearing clothing, entertaining, or even just opening the daily mail in your home results in something to be thrown out, washed, or put away. Even if you're away on vacation, the dust still settles. Housekeeping is a chore that never ends. However, that doesn't mean it needs to be a drudgery that continually weighs you down. Simplifying the housekeeping in your life begins with putting it in the proper perspective.

Jesus helped his friend Martha do just that. When Jesus dropped by for a visit, Luke 10:40 (NIV) explains that Martha was "distracted by all the preparations that had to be made." Furthermore, Martha was not too pleased that her sister Mary wasn't lending a hand. However, Jesus encouraged Martha not to worry or be upset over what had to be done. He told her one thing was needed, not several. One thing she could have done herself and still had time to listen to Jesus.

If Jesus dropped by for a visit today, chances are you'd automatically drop everything to spend time with him, but you might wish you'd taken a couple of minutes to hide the dirty laundry. Nevertheless, Jesus' point remains— people are more important than presentation. That doesn't mean you should let your house become a trash heap. The Bible encourages you to take care of what you own. What it means is that you should care more about making people feel welcome than about impressing them with your freshly buffed floor.

Less is more when it comes to housekeeping. Choosing to simplify the maintenance required in your home makes it easier to put people first. Having fewer possessions means less to put away. And when it comes to putting things away, picking up after yourself when you use something keeps the time you spend cleaning house to a minimum.

ONE FINAL THOUGHT

Housekeeping is less of a chore once you've picked up a godly perspective about its importance in life.

Thoughts for Living Simply

The Lord blesses the home of the righteous.
Proverbs 3:33 NIV

Let there be no disappointment when obedience keeps you busy in out-
ward tasks. If it sends you to the kitchen, remember that the Lord walks
among the pots and pans.
Saint Theresa of Avila

Make it your ambition to lead a quiet life, to mind your own
business and to work with your hands, just as we told you, so
that your daily life may win the respect of outsiders and so that
you will not be dependent on anybody.
1 Thessalonians 4:11–12 NIV

Happiness is to be found only in the home where God is loved and hon-
oured, where each one loves, and helps, and cares
for the others.
Theophanes Vénard

Remember...

_____Jesus urged Martha to simplicity.

_____Complicated house-work simply complicates your life.

_____God asks you to give thanks in everything, and that includes cleaning the kitchen.

_____Jesus washed his disciples' feet, and you, too, can be a servant to those you love by helping clean up after them.

Simplify...

Turn repetitive chores, such as washing dishes or doing laundry, into a special time to talk to God.

Buy all-purpose cleaners, so you only have one spray bottle to carry with you as you clean.

Purchase cookware with a non-stick coating for easy cleanup.

Keep knickknacks to a minimum so you have less to dust.

Make housecleaning day a celebration. Tune in to a contemporary Christian radio station and sing while you work.

By wisdom a house is built, and through understanding it is established.
Proverbs 24:3 NIV

SOMETIMES YOU'VE GOT TO GET HELP

If I have been able to see farther than others, it is because
I have stood on the shoulders of giants.

Sir Isaac Newton

There are times when all it takes is one word to simplify
your life. That word is help. Consider trying to move a large
sofa. You could try tackling the job on your own with ropes,
pulleys, and good, old-fashioned brute force. After consider-
able time and effort, you may even be able to accomplish the
task. But you will have significantly complicated your life,
and maybe even hurt yourself.

You know it's ridiculous to not enlist the aid of a couple
of friends to move something too heavy to budge alone.
However, some "sofas" in this life are not quite as
obvious as those of the furniture persuasion. Perhaps
you're putting in another weekend at the office
instead of asking your boss for some administra-
tive support. Or maybe you are trying to do all
the housework alone
instead of getting
your kids more
involved so you
can accomplish more

64

of what you need to do during the day. Or perhaps you are trying to carry an emotional burden that you just can't seem to unload by yourself instead of turning to a friend, pastor, or counselor. Or maybe you are trying to live this life on your own and you need to admit to God that you just can't.

When God created the world, he said it wasn't good for people to be alone. God created people for community. That means you were created to be interdependent with those around you and not self-sufficient. You were also created to be dependent on God. While it's true God will never give you more than you can handle, he'll often give you more than you can handle on your own.

Calling on God and those around you for assistance when you need it will make your life simpler as well as help you accomplish things you could never do by yourself. Admitting you need help is a sign of wisdom and humility. It can also help open your eyes to how you, in turn, can reach out and lend others a hand when they are in need of help.

ONE FINAL THOUGHT

Asking for help when you need it not only lightens your load, but also gives others the opportunity to express their love by serving you.

Thoughts for Living Simply

Two are better off than one, because together they can work more effectively. If one of them falls down, the other can help him up. But if someone is alone and falls, it's just too bad, because there is no one to help him. If it is cold, two can sleep together and stay warm, but how can you keep warm by yourself? Two people can resist an attack that would defeat one person alone. A rope made of three cords is hard to break.

Ecclesiastes 4:9–12 GNT

We must support one another, console one another, mutually help, counsel, and advise.

Thomas à Kempis

Carry each other's burdens, and in this way you will fulfill the law of Christ.

Galatians 6:2 NIV

It is one of the beautiful compensations of this life that no one can sincerely try to help another without helping himself.

Charles Dudley Warner

Remember...

_____Jesus asked his disciples to help him minister to those in need.

_____Love is often most visible through a helping hand.

_____Being dependent on one another is one way God builds community.

_____God will often use those around you to answer your prayers to him for help.

Simplify...

Get involved in a small group at your church so you can help others and they can help you.

Accept the assistance others offer you with gratitude and humility.

Ask God to help you discern when and who to ask for help.

Look at your life and identify areas where others could help you, like with housework or yard work.

Share your own prayer requests openly and ask for help when you need it.

There can't be blessed givers if there aren't blessed receivers.
Ben Campbell Johnson

TAMING THE WILD CLOTHESHORSE

The Lord does not look at the things man looks at. Man looks at the outward appearance, but the Lord looks at the heart.

I Samuel 16:7 NIV

When Adam and Eve first felt the need to cover themselves, they grabbed whatever they had on hand to do the job. Today your choices of what to wear are greater than what happens to be growing in your yard. As time goes by, a little shopping here and a few Christmas gifts there can make your closet in desperate need of pruning, even without the fig leaves.

Pruning your wardrobe should begin outside your closet door. While modesty and weather play a big part in determining your wardrobe, so can vanity, peer pressure, and even greed if you let them. Checking your motives, along with the trendiness of your clothing, is one positive step toward a simpler life. If you try to prune your wardrobe without attending to what's growing in your heart, the changes you make will only be temporary. Unchecked insecurities can refill a recently pruned closet in no time.

Take a good long look at what you wear and why. What motivates you to purchase an outfit? Do you really believe you are exactly the same person whether you're wearing stained sweatpants or a tailored suit by Versace? Other people may perceive you differently, but clothes do not determine who you really are. Your identity is found in Christ alone.

Compared to matters of the heart, downsizing your actual wardrobe is easy. (The Simplify section offers you a few helpful hints to get you started.) Intentionally pruning your wardrobe will simplify your life by giving you more space, both in your closet and your schedule. It will provide you with fewer choices to make, decreased maintenance, and less clutter.

For choosing what to put on each morning, the Bible offers some eternal fashion tips. It says to clothe "yourself with compassion, kindness, humility, gentleness, and patience" (Colossians 3:12 NIV) and "with the Lord Jesus Christ" (Romans 13:14 NIV).

ONE FINAL THOUGHT

Once you clothe yourself with humility, everything else you put on seems a little less important.

Thoughts for Living Simply

Jesus said, "Why do you worry about clothes? See how the wild flowers grow. They don't work or make clothing. But here is what I tell you. Not even Solomon in all of his glory was dressed like one of those flowers."
Matthew 6:28–29 NIRV

He is ill clothed that is bare of virtue.
Benjamin Franklin

Your beauty should not come from outward adornment, such as braided hair and the wearing of gold jewelry and fine clothes. Instead, it should be that of your inner self, the unfading beauty of a gentle and quiet spirit, which is of great worth in God's sight.
1 Peter 3:3–4 NIV

Let thy attire be comely, but not costly.
John Lyly

Remember...

_____Jesus and his disciples had no luggage.

_____God looks at your heart rather than at the label on your clothes.

_____The less time you spend getting ready every morning, the more time you have to spend with God.

_____Love coordinates perfectly with any outfit you choose to wear.

Simplify...

Throw out or give away what you haven't worn in over a year.

Mend any clothing that needs fixing so that whatever you choose is ready to wear.

Keep to a minimum clothing that needs to be ironed, dry-cleaned, or hand-washed.

Buy clothes to replace items that wear out rather than to expand your options.

Choose classic items you'll enjoy for years over trendy fashions you'll wear for a season.

When God measures a person, he puts the tape measure around the heart.
Dennis Faltis

EVERY SEASON IS A CELEBRATION

"Even to your old age and gray hairs I am he, I am he who will sustain you. I have made you and I will carry you; I will sustain you and I will rescue you," says the Lord.

Isaiah 46:4 NIV

Every season has a beauty all its own. From winter's snowfall to the first buds of spring, summer-ripened strawberries to a canopy of fall colors, it's hard to choose which season is best. Perhaps the fact that seasons change is one important aspect of their beauty. If your life became perpetual summer, chances are you'd lose some of your appreciation of sunny afternoons and long for a cooling breeze every now and again.

Like the natural world, your body experiences various seasons of life. But there's one season most people want to hold on to dearly—youth. The problem is, seasons change and so do people. Trying to hold on to youth is like an apple tree trying to retain its beautiful spring blossoms. If its efforts did succeed, it would miss out on bearing fruit.

Your body is an impermanent dwelling place that God created

for the real you to live in while you're here on earth. But it's a temporary structure. The good news is that while your body is aging, the real you inside is maturing. It's becoming more beautiful as the years pass by. God's spirit and your life experience are rounding off some of your rough edges and polishing some of your finer points to an even more attractive finish.

Accepting and even learning to appreciate this process is one way to simplify your life. Trying to wear the same size you did in high school, keeping your hair from looking gray, or creating the illusion that your skin is immune to wrinkles takes time, energy, and resources. It also encourages you to gauge some of your self-worth on your appearance, which gives other people's opinions too much weight in your life. Keep in mind that every season has its own unique merit. Learning to accept the season you and your body are in—and revel in it—will make every time of your life more beautiful and less stressful.

ONE FINAL THOUGHT

Every age has its own unique beauty and potential for growth.

Thoughts for Living Simply

There is a time for everything, and a season for every activity under heaven.

Ecclesiastes 3:1 NIV

Life is the childhood of our immortality.

Johann Wolfgang von Goethe

The glory of youths is their strength; but the beauty of the aged is their gray hair.

Proverbs 20:29 NRSV

Youth is not a time of life; it is a state of mind; it is not a matter of rosy cheeks, red lips and supple knees; it is a matter of the will, a quality of the imagination, a vigor of the emotions; it is the freshness of the deep springs of life.

Samuel Ullman

Remember...

_____Inner beauty never wrinkles.

_____Every birthday should be a celebration of personal growth and a cause for personal delight.

_____Christ saw beauty in children, lepers, prostitutes, and an old woman who gave all she had.

_____The best facelift and spirit lifter is a smile.

Simplify...

Buy the size that fits, regardless of what size you wish you were.

Get your hair cut in a flattering, low-maintenance style that you can simply wash and wear.

Cut down how much time you spend looking in the mirror.

Appreciate who you are—brag about your age.

Make a mental list of what you enjoy about being the age you are now, and thank God for everything that comes to mind.

Nothing makes one old so quickly as the ever-present thought that one is growing older.
Georg Christoph Lichtenberg

THE CONTENTMENT OF A
THANKFUL HEART

Thou that has given so much to me, give one thing
more—a grateful heart; not thankful when it pleaseth me,
as if thy blessings had spare days; but such a heart, whose
pulse may be thy praise.
George Herbert

Thanks be to God, who in Christ always leads us in tri-
umphal procession, and through us spreads in every place
the fragrance that comes from knowing him.
2 Corinthians 2:14 NRSV

Give thanks to the Lord, proclaim his greatness; tell the
nations what he has done. Sing praise to the Lord; tell
the wonderful things he has done. Be glad that we belong
to him; let all who worship him rejoice! Go to the Lord
for help, and worship him continually.
1 Chronicles 16:8–11 GNT

Let us give thanks to God! He wins the battle for us
because of what our Lord Jesus Christ has done.
1 Corinthians 15:57 NIRV

Not more of light I ask, O God,
But eyes to see what is:
Not sweeter songs, but ears to hear
The present melodies.
Not more of strength, but how to use
The power I possess:
Not more of love, but skill to turn
A frown to a caress:
Not more of joy, but how to feel
Its kindly presence near
To give to others all I have
Of courage and of cheer.

No other gifts, dear God, I ask,
But only sense to see
How best these precious gifts to use
Thou has bestowed on me.
Author Unknown

THE TREASURE MAP OF A PAPER PLAN

There is a time for everything . . . a time to search and a time to give up,
a time to keep and a time to throw away.

Ecclesiastes 3:1, 6 NIV

Searching for buried treasure is often regarded as a
swashbuckling adventure. It's more frustrating than fun,
however, when the buried treasure you're searching for is an
important document lost in a paper pile of who-knows-what.
That's why having a plan to keep paper clutter from taking
over your home or office is its own kind of treasure map. It
can lead you right to important papers when you need them,
thereby simplifying your life.

In biblical times, as now, important papers had to be
protected and kept secure. The scrolls of the Law—Genesis,
Exodus, Leviticus, Numbers, and Deuteronomy—
were sacred and precious, and they were
kept in the Ark of the Covenant. The
Ark was a sacred box, protecting
the tablets from being lost or
damaged. "After Moses finished
writing in a book the words
of this law from beginning to

end, he gave this command to the Levites who carried the ark of the covenant of the Lord: 'Take this Book of the Law and place it beside the ark of the covenant of the Lord your God. There it will remain as a witness against you'" (Deuteronomy 31:24–26).

That same care should be taken with your important documents. Though no paper in your possession is as valuable as the Ten Commandments, items such as birth certificates, deeds, passports, and stock certificates should be kept in a safe-deposit box. Other important financial papers, including tax documents, bank statements, and bills, are most easily organized with a simple filing system.

Part of protecting your important papers is deciding what is worth protecting. The first time you handle a piece of paper, decide whether you need to act on it, file it, or get rid of it. Choosing to deal with it later is the first step toward making a pile. Fight that urge! Save time, and a potentially unpleasant treasure hunt, by making a decision. Then follow through with it.

ONE FINAL THOUGHT

Any paper worth saving is worth filing, so you can find it when you need it.

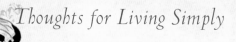

Thoughts for Living Simply

Do not forsake wisdom, and she will protect you; love her, and
she will watch over you.
Proverbs 4:6 NIV

There is a better way for everything. Find it.
Thomas Edison

Rejoice in the Lord! It is no trouble for me to write the same
things to you again, and it is a safeguard for you.
Philippians 3:1 NIV

*I love order. It's my dream. A world where all would be silent and still
and each thing in its last place, under the last dust.*
Samuel Beckett

Remember...

_____God's love of order is evident in all he has created.

_____The efficacy of using your time wisely honors God.

_____The less clutter there is in your life, the less there is to distract you from what's most important.

_____Small tasks accomplished today save you from doing tougher tasks tomorrow.

Simplify...

Throw out or give away magazines and catalogs as soon as you are finished reading them.

Clean out your purse or wallet at least once a week and file what is of value.

Put any recipes clipped from the paper or given to you by friends into a self-adhesive photo album or input or scan them into your computer.

Open your mail next to the wastebasket and throw away junk mail unopened.

I discovered an easy way to help people improve their productivity:
Clean off the pile of papers on the desk.
Jeffrey J. Mayer

FATHER STILL KNOWS BEST

This is love for God: to obey his commands.

1 John 5:3 NIV

Scrub your teeth. Do your homework. Wear a jacket when it's cold. Put your toys away. Share. Childhood is filled with rules. When children obey the rules, life is simpler for their parents, teachers, and even their playmates. But until children grow into adulthood, most of them won't fully comprehend how following the rules simplified their own lives.

Scrubbing their teeth helped prevent cavities. Doing their homework improved their chances of succeeding in school and beyond. Wearing a jacket kept them from getting sick in inclement weather. Putting their toys away prevented their possessions from getting lost or broken. Sharing helped build relationships. The reward for obedience was far more than just avoiding punishment. Following the rules actually made life easier.

Obedience holds the same benefits for adults that it does for kids. It keeps you out of trouble and makes daily life run more smoothly. As an adult, you've outgrown your need for your parents' wisdom in setting up rules to run your life, but you'll never outgrow your need for the rules God has provided.

If you haven't taken a look at the Ten Commandments in a while, read them in a contemporary version of the Bible, such as the NIrV or Good News Translation. But don't stop there. Obey what they say. Doing so will simplify your life. For instance, if you steal or murder, you may end up in prison and cloud your future with regret. If you accuse anyone falsely, you may destroy a relationship as well as your reputation. Following God's rules prevents these things from happening. Obeying the Ten Commandments also draws you closer to God and others.

Choosing to put yourself under someone else's authority, even God's, isn't easy or natural. But choosing to be obedient in both big and small things will draw you more deeply into the beautiful life adventure God has planned for you.

ONE FINAL THOUGHT

Obedience is the key that opens the door to God's very best in your life.

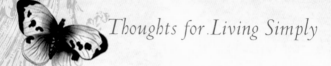

Thoughts for Living Simply

Obey your leaders and submit to their authority. They keep watch over you as men who must give an account. Obey them so that their work will be a joy.

Hebrews 13:17 NIV

I know the power obedience has of making things easy which seem impossible.

Saint Theresa of Avila

What pleases the Lord more? Burnt offerings and sacrifices, or obeying him? It is better to obey than to offer a sacrifice.

1 Samuel 15:22 NIRV

Happy the soul which, by a sincere self-renunciation, holds itself ceaselessly in the hands of its Creator, ready to do everything which He wishes; which never stops saying to itself a hundred times a day, "Lord, what would you have me do?"

François de La Mothe Fénelon

Remember...

_____God gave the Ten Commandments to be followed, not the Ten Suggestions to be considered.

_____Jesus' obedience to his Father focused and simplified his life.

_____The Gospel of Luke says that Jesus was obedient to his earthly parents, as well as his heavenly Father.

_____Obedience simplifies decision making.

Simplify...

Obey the posted speed limits and you won't have to worry about getting a ticket for speeding.

Honor God by honoring your mother and father, no matter what your age.

If you always tell the truth, you won't have to remember as much.

Be truthful in filing out your tax forms, obeying God's command not to steal.

Ask God to reveal to you any areas in your life where you could grow in loving obedience.

In obeying, a rational creature consciously enacts its creaturely role, reverses the act by which we fell, treads Adam's dance backwards, and returns.

C. S. Lewis

FOOD FOR THOUGHT

To God who gives our daily bread a thankful song we raise, and pray that he who sends us food may fill our hearts with praise.

Thomas Tallis

The question "What's for dinner?" would be simpler to answer if God provided manna every day for us to dine on. However, God is both generous and creative. He has supplied ingredients for everything from apple dumplings to zabaglione custard. But deciding what you want to eat is only the first step. Next you need to purchase the ingredients, prepare the meal, consume it, and finally, clean up after it. All in all, dining three times a day is an activity that could use a little simplification.

Jesus and his disciples planned a time of retreat, but word went ahead of them. When their boat landed on the beach, thousands of people were waiting, eager for Jesus' healing. Jesus had compassion and healed many. But the day grew late, and the disciples were concerned about the need for the people to eat. Jesus gave a simple directive. "Give them something to eat," he said. Then

86

the disciples were even more concerned—they had only five loaves of bread and two fish. But Jesus told the people to sit down, and he took the provisions and blessed them. All ate and were satisfied, and twelve baskets of food were left over.

When faced with an impromptu dinner party of several thousand people, Jesus kept it simple. He took what he had on hand—a few loaves of bread and a couple of fish. He thanked his father for the food, and then shared what he had with those around him. Afterward, his disciples picked up the leftovers. What a marvelous lesson in simplicity and efficiency in using the resources at your disposal.

Before you head to the grocery store, consider Jesus' example. He served simple, healthy food. He was thankful for what God had provided. He knew the value of leftovers. Consider what you need nutritionally, what you can afford financially, and what you have time to prepare realistically. Make a list and stick to it. Work leftovers into your weekly menu. Then prepare and eat what you've purchased with a thankful heart.

One Final Thought

To eat healthily, you need to plan thoughtfully.

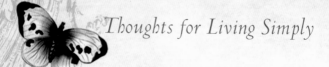

Thoughts for Living Simply

Taking the five loaves and the two fish, Jesus looked up to heaven, and blessed and broke the loaves, and gave them to the disciples, and the disciples gave them to the crowds. And all ate and were filled; and they took up what was left over of the broken pieces, twelve baskets full. And those who ate were about five thousand men, besides women and children.

Matthew 14:19–21 NRSV

Food ought to be a refreshment for the body and not a burden.
Saint Bonaventure

Better to eat a dry crust of bread with peace of mind than have a banquet in a house full of trouble.
Proverbs 17:1 GNT

As to different kinds of food, we should take a little of everything, even sweets . . . We should never pick and choose, or push our food aside, but should thank God for everything.
Nilus Sorsky

Remember...

_____God has generously
provided a variety of food.

_____Good food can often
be prepared from what you
have on hand.

_____Jesus set a good ex-
ample of being creative with
what you have.

_____Working leftovers into
your meal planning saves
cooking time.

Simplify...

*Keep a list of available snack and
meal options on the refrigerator
door, to remind you of what you
have on hand.*

*Double recipes and freeze half for
an easy meal later.*

*When planning a recipe that
requires only half of an ingredient
you don't usually buy, plan to
prepare another recipe that will
use the other half.*

*Use coupons only if they save you
more money than the time you
spend clipping them is worth.*

*Starting off to Death Valley unprovisioned may seem foolish, but
Elijah made a remarkable rediscovery. God himself serves the meals
to a man in his service.*
David A. Redding

Being a Living Stone, I Presume?

Since you are eager to have spiritual gifts, try to excel in gifts that build up the church.

1 Corinthians 14:12 NIV

"This is the church and this is the steeple. Open the door and see all the people." This children's finger play, where you get to wiggle your intertwined fingers in such a way as to make the people inside the church sway with delight, is only half right. The church is not only the building that holds the people, but the church is also the people within the building. The church building may protect the people from the elements outside, but the church community protects the people inside by offering spiritual, emotional, and physical support, as well as providing special services such as weddings, baptisms, and funerals. Members of the church community use their gifts to serve one another.

The book of Acts gives a picture of how the very first church community helped simplify people's lives. Those who were familiar with Jesus' teachings shared what they knew with others, helping them grow spiritually. As the first Christians were being persecuted, the church community prayed and provided emotional support. Members of the church also pooled their resources, so they were able to offer necessities like food and shelter to those in need. This church had no building. Instead, it was built from living stones, people who built into each other's lives by sharing of themselves.

Choosing to get involved in a church community helps simplify your life by enabling you to do more than you could do on your own. Involvement requires participation in the church's ministries—contributing to and benefiting from the church's fellowship, knowledge, and resources.

Being part of a church is more than being served by others. It is an opportunity for you use your unique, God-given gifts to simplify the lives of others as well as your own. Examples of these opportunities are choir, food pantry, visitation, greeters, altar guild, and many more. Sunday morning is just the beginning. Even when the church building is closed, God's Church is open.

ONE FINAL THOUGHT

The church community is made up of unique individuals who help simplify each other's lives by using their gifts to serve one another.

Thoughts for Living Simply

[The believers] devoted themselves to the apostles' teaching and
to the fellowship, to the breaking of bread and to prayer.
Acts 2:42 NIV

*Now the church is not wood and stone, but the company of people who
believe in Christ.*
Martin Luther

Let us consider how to stimulate one another to love and good
deeds, not forsaking our own assembling together, as is the
habit of some, but encouraging one another; and all the more as
you see the day drawing near.
Hebrews 10:24–25 NASB

*You cannot pray at home as at church, where there is a great multitude,
where exclamations are cried out to God as from one great heart, and
where there is something more: the union of minds, the accord of souls,
the bond of charity, the prayers of priests.*
Saint John Chrysostom

Remember...

_____Jesus said that where two or three people gathered together, he would be right there with them.

_____Churches are made up of imperfect people being perfected by a flawless God.

_____The need to serve others is as strong as the desire to be served.

_____Your church is incomplete without you.

Simplify...

If you attend a large church, join a small group rather than trying to get to know many people.

Maintain a godly balance of serving and being served in your church community.

Take a spiritual gifts test to help you determine where you fit best in serving your church.

Ask for help from your church when you need it.

Keep your group meetings or dinners simple, focusing on God and fellowship rather than on elaborate programs or meals.

The Church is Christ existing as community.
Dietrich Bonhoeffer

MAKING THE MOST OF THE MOMENT

Nothing valuable can be lost by taking time.
Abraham Lincoln

"Simplify your life by making the best use of your time. You can accomplish this by becoming more organized, procrastinating less, or planning ahead. But there's another way to make the most of your time that has nothing to do with becoming more efficient. It has to do with slowing down the pace of your life.

Imagine two people who have each won a yearlong trip around the world. One of them decides to cram in as many cities as possible. He spends the night in 365 different locations, flying out each morning to a new locale. The second chooses the top twelve countries she's always wanted to visit. She spends a month exploring each country by car, train, and ferry, choosing to spend more or less time at each location according to her interests. Which person do you feel has made the most of his or her time?

The answer is not black-and-white. However, chances are that the woman with the slower itinerary will remember more about individual destinations, will have started relationships along the way, and will return more physically and mentally refreshed than the fellow on the whirlwind tour.

When Jesus promised you an abundant life, he meant that each day of your life would be filled more completely with what mattered—love, joy, and peace. When life speeds up, and every moment is filled with tasks demanding to be accomplished before bedtime, it is easy to miss what God has set aside for you to enjoy along the way.

Each new day is a once-in-a-lifetime experience. Slowing down to savor the little things—a blazing sunset, a chance meeting with a friend, a kiss on the cheek from someone you love—will help you make every moment count toward a more abundant life.

ONE FINAL THOUGHT

The abundant life and the simple life are synonymous when each moment is filled with only God's best.

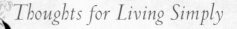

Thoughts for Living Simply

Teach us to count our days.
Psalm 90:12 NRSV

The value of life lies not in the length of days but in the use you make of them.
Michel de Montaigne

This is the day the Lord has made; we will rejoice and be glad in it.
Psalm 118:24 NKJV

Carry your wishes to their furthest limits, open your heart boundlessly, there is not a single moment when you will not find all you could possibly desire. The present moment holds infinite riches beyond your wildest dreams.
Jean-Pierre de Caussade

Remember...

_____Moments can be filled with joy and purpose, without being filled with activity.

_____God is never in a hurry.

_____A blender does certain jobs best on slow speed—the same is true of you.

_____You only get one chance to spend the present moment—invest it in something of eternal worth.

Simplify...

Pray about the pace of your life and ask God to reveal any changes you need to make.

Do one thing at a time, giving whatever is at hand your undivided attention.

Leave for work, church, or ballgame on time and drive the speed limit, enjoying the journey by singing along with the radio or talking to God.

Resist the temptation to stay in high gear all day long, whether at work, at home, or even on vacation.

Until you value yourself, you won't value your time. Until you value your time, you will not do anything with it.
M. Scott Peck

THE POWER OF PERSPECTIVE

Lord, purge our eyes to see within the seed a tree, within the glowing egg a bird, within the shroud a butterfly, till, taught by such, we see beyond all creatures, thee.
Christina Rosetti

What this world considers to be wisdom is nonsense in God's sight.
1 Corinthians 3:19 GNT

Open my eyes so that I can see the wonderful truths in your law.
Psalm 119:18 NIRV

Set your minds on things that are in heaven, where Christ sits on his throne at the right side of God. Keep your minds fixed on things there, not on things here on earth. For you have died, and your life is hidden with Christ in God. Your real life is Christ.
Colossians 3:1–4 GNT

You, dear children, are from God . . . the one who is

in you is greater than the one who is in the world.

[False prophets] are from the world and therefore

speak from the viewpoint of the world, and the

world listens to them. We are from God, and who-

ever knows God listens to us; but whoever is not

from God does not listen to us.

This is how we recognize the Spirit of truth

and the spirit of falsehood.

1 John 4:4–6 NIV

THE TIME TO ACT IS NOW

Procrastination makes easy things hard, hard things harder.
Mason Cooley

The day ahead promises to be busy. Your schedule is full. Your to-do list is spilling onto a second page. But there are a few items at the bottom of the list that were there yesterday, as well as the day before, the week before, maybe even the month before. Procrastination complicates your life. You keep telling yourself that you work best under pressure, but the fact is that when tomorrow's to-do list comes around, all procrastination has bought you is more stress.

Accomplishing what needs to be done today instead of putting it off until tomorrow or indefinitely helps your life run more smoothly. While procrastinating may seem to save you time today, all it really does is force a delayed task into the schedule of some day down the road. So why does anyone procrastinate? It could be the desire to avoid the unpleasant (making an embarrassing apology, gathering documentation for taxes, preparing for a meeting you'd rather not attend), or it could be an overloaded schedule or a touch of laziness.

Felix's procrastination had a serious consequence. Felix, who was governor at the time of Paul, listened to the apostle talk about Jesus, but he delayed a decision. "As Paul went on discussing about goodness, self-control, and the coming Day of Judgment, Felix was afraid and said, 'You may leave now. I will call you again when I get the chance'" (Acts 24:25 GNT). Unfortunately, Felix died a short time later.

If there's something you've been putting off, face it head on. Once a week, choose to do one thing you've been procrastinating over. Before you know it, the weight of what's been left undone will be lifted off your shoulders—and off your to-do list.

ONE FINAL THOUGHT

Facing today's tasks today keeps tomorrow more available to God's precious possibilities.

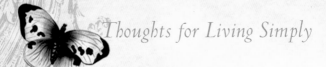
Thoughts for Living Simply

In everything that [Hezekiah] undertook in the service of
God's temple and in obedience to the law and the commands,
he sought his God and worked wholeheartedly. And so he
prospered.

2 Chronicles 31:21 NIV

*When you have to make a choice and don't make it, that in itself is a
choice.*

William James

Moses said to the people, "Do not be afraid, stand firm, and see
the deliverance that the Lord will accomplish for you today; for
the Egyptians whom you see today you shall never see again.
The Lord will fight for you; and you have only to keep still."

Exodus 14:13–14 NRSV

*Know the true value of time. Snatch, seize, and enjoy every moment of
it. No idleness, no laziness, no procrastination. Never put off till tomorrow what you can do today.*

Lord Chesterfield

Remember...

_____Procrastination only brings more stress when tomorrow comes around.

_____God discourages procrastination by asking that you never let the sun go down before you amend angry words (see Ephesians 4:26).

_____Working through a to-do list of procrastinated actions will gradually lift the weight from your shoulders.

_____With God, you never tackle unpleasant tasks alone.

Simplify...

Face unpleasant tasks on your daily to-do list first, so you'll be less likely to procrastinate.

Get in the habit of scheduling your annual physical every January so you'll do it on a regular basis.

Attend to rented videos, library books, and bills on time by writing due dates in your planner as a reminder.

Pray for perseverance in accomplishing tasks you would rather postpone.

Ask God for wisdom any time you are tempted to procrastinate, and ask for help in breaking that cycle.

Indecision is the thief of opportunity.
Jim Rohn

LIFE'S REJUVENATION STATION

God is our refuge and strength, a very present help in trouble.

Psalm 46:1 NRSV

The word retreat might bring to mind a vintage Hollywood war movie. In the din of the battlefield, the officer desires to maximize the possibility for success. Signaling for the bugle to be sounded, the officer leads his troops back from the battle into safety. He has ordered a strategic retreat to make new plans.

There are times when you also need to retreat to rest and plan strategy. Scheduling regular personal retreats is a proactive step that allows you to evaluate activities, refocus on priorities, plan, and recharge. You first take stock of what condition you are already in, and you reflect. You then establish a plan to develop needed skills and strength and make practical plans to strengthen any areas of weakness. You spend time in prayer and Bible study, getting acquainted with how others have faced challenges in the past. When the day comes to put your plan into action, the challenge is much easier than it would have been had you not prepared yourself.

Before Jesus tackled the challenge of his ministry on earth, he retreated to the desert for forty days. Through fasting and prayer, Jesus was mentally and spiritually prepared to face the temptations he encountered there, as well as ready to begin the most difficult three years of his life. Throughout his ministry, he continued to make smaller retreats as needed.

You don't have to fast for forty days to take a personal retreat. Setting aside at least a two-hour block of time every month and one full day a year for prayerful reflection and planning should be adequate to help you get in shape for the relational, vocational, physical, emotional, and spiritual challenges that may lie ahead.

A retreat is a time to reflect on the past and plan for the future. Evaluate your strengths and weaknesses. Dream big dreams. With God's guidance, make a game plan.

ONE FINAL THOUGHT

Regular retreats will give you the strength you need to charge ahead with confidence.

Thoughts for Living Simply

Draw near to God and He will draw near to you.
James 4:8 NASB

A humble knowledge of oneself is a surer road to God than a deep searching of the sciences.
Thomas à Kempis

God gives me strength for the battle. He makes my way perfect. He makes my feet like the feet of a deer. He helps me stand on the highest places. He trains my hands to fight every battle. My arms can bend a bow of bronze. Lord, you are like a shield that keeps me safe. You help me win the battle. You bend down to make me great.
2 Samuel 22:33–36 NIRV

My great concern is not whether God is on our side, my great concern is to be on God's side.
Abraham Lincoln

Remember...

_____A retreat is a spiritual tool for preparing to meet a challenge.

_____God and the Bible make the best mirror for personal reflection.

_____A retreat affords an excellent opportunity to reflect on the past and plan for the future.

_____God can only be your refuge if you choose to retreat to his presence.

Simplify...

Write down whatever God reveals to you so you can review it during future times of retreat, and include the following strategies:

Schedule the time and find a quiet spot with minimal distractions for your retreat.

Treat time for your personal retreat just as you would any other appointment—schedule it in advance and postpone only if necessary.

Take action on whatever God reveals to you.

Go off, find a place alone, and listen to the Lord.
Todd Wetzel

A Perfect Fit

In this world people honor the brilliant; people honor different achievements without realizing that all these were gifts of God.

Eagle Vision Ministry

You are an individual piece of a puzzle that spans eternity. You have a specific shape and form. This includes the color of your skin, the curve of your smile, the contours of your heart. God has placed within you certain passions, abilities, and personality traits. Your exclusive design enables you to perfectly fill the spot God has set apart for you. That's why finding and filling the right spot helps simplify your life because it fits the way you were made. That spot is where your talents can best be put to use and where you can avoid the friction of trying to squeeze yourself into the wrong space.

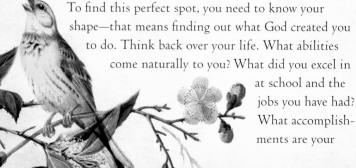

To find this perfect spot, you need to know your shape—that means finding out what God created you to do. Think back over your life. What abilities come naturally to you? What did you excel in at school and the jobs you have had? What accomplishments are your most proud of? What did you dream of doing? Ask God to help you find your talents and gifts in all of life.

By discovering the spiritual gifts and abilities that God gave you, you may come to understand why you have a longing for adventure, an interest in science, a fascination with complex mechanical equipment, or the need to do something that will make a difference in the world. And you may learn how God desires that you act on these penchants.

Keeping your vocation, hobbies, and ability to reach out to others in line with your individual passions and personality will save you from the frustration and ineffectiveness of that square-peg-in-a-round-hole feeling. And it will enable you to fill to the best of your potential your God-given place in this world.

ONE FINAL THOUGHT

Living up to your potential begins with discovering and embracing who God created you to be.

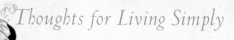

Thoughts for Living Simply

I praise you, for I am fearfully and wonderfully made. Wonderful are your works; that I know very well. My frame was not hidden from you, when I was being made in secret, intricately woven in the depths of the earth. Your eyes beheld my unformed substance. In your book were written all the days that were formed for me, when none of them as yet existed.
Psalm 139:14–16 NRSV

The spirit's presence is shown in some way in each person for the good of all.
1 Corinthians 12:7 GNT

We are God's workmanship, created in Christ Jesus to do good works, which God prepared in advance for us to do.
Ephesians 2:10 NIV

Use what talents you possess: the woods would be very silent if no birds sang there except those that sang best.
Henry Van Dyke

Remember...

_____No one except you can
fill the spot God has prepared for you.

_____Using God's gifts pleases him in the same way that enjoying a birthday gift you've been given brings joy to the one who gave it to you.

_____There are many different abilities but all are given by God.

_____Jesus had a special spot in history that he filled perfectly.

Simplify...

Ask those who know you well what they believe are your most apparent God-given gifts.

Review any temperament tests you have taken for employment to better understand your abilities.

List the five most fulfilling experiences you've had and evaluate why you feel passionate about them.

With prayer, planning, and counsel from those who know you best, risk moving out of a spot that is not right for you.

Now you are the body of Christ, and each one of you is a part of it.
1 Corinthians 12:27 NIV

111

Being a Wait Watcher

I waited patiently for the Lord; he turned to me and heard my cry.

Psalm 40:1 NIV

Some areas of life will always be out of your control. You can choose the shortest route for your evening commute, for instance, and still be delayed by a traffic jam on the way home. You can put all of the self-control you can muster into trying to speak only kind words, and yet still hear a negative comment slip through your lips. When it comes to situations beyond your control, living the simple life becomes synonymous with learning the patient life.

Growth of any kind takes time. But learning to be patient with yourself, as well as with others, frees you to enjoy the natural pace of life, which at times can be slower than you'd like it to be. Practicing patience is choosing to ask God to reveal what he wants to teach you while you're waiting. Does he want you to learn to forgive others when they make mistakes? Does he want you to learn to find joy in the journey, even when you find yourself living in the slow lane?

When Jesus died, his followers were in limbo for three days, waiting and wondering what would happen. When Jesus heard Lazarus was sick, he waited until after Lazarus had died to show up to help his friend. God led the Israelites to wander in the desert for forty years on a journey that should have taken only a short time. God's timetable often seems to be one that encourages the growth of patience. Waiting for God helps relieve stress by putting things in perspective.

Think of why you get impatient. Perhaps you want your own way, you are too busy, or you are not looking from God's perspective. Patience slows you down enough to help you find the lessons hidden behind inconveniences. It helps remind you that God is ultimately in control. Patience takes the pressure off of you to make things happen according to your plan and allows you to mature by accepting the preeminence of God's plan. The more patience grows in you, the less physical tension you'll find building inside you when the unexpected happens.

One Final Thought

When God's timing differs from your own, patience keeps you from trying to control something that is out of your hands.

Thoughts for Living Simply

With the Lord a day is like a thousand years, and a thousand years are like a day. The Lord is not slow in keeping his promises, as some understand slowness. He is patient with you, not wanting anyone to perish, but everyone to come to repentance.
2 Peter 3:8–9 NIV

Obedience is the fruit of faith; patience, the bloom on the fruit.
Christina Rossetti

May you be made strong with all the strength which comes from his glorious power, so that you may be able to endure everything with patience.
Colossians 1:11 GNT

In the rush and noise of life, as you have intervals, step within yourselves and be still. Wait upon God and feel his good presence; this will carry you through your day's business.
William Penn

Remember...

_____God's timing is always perfect, and waiting helps you see things from God's perspective.

_____Seemingly unanswered prayers make excellent teachers for learning the art of patience.

_____God's timetable often encourages patience and cultivates simple living.

_____The best way to wait is with your eyes and heart wide open.

Simplify...

Try to build flexibility into your schedule to deal with the unexpected.

Practice patience by letting others go ahead of you in line at the grocery store.

Pray for the drivers around you when you get stuck in traffic; notice how this relieves tension from a potentially stress-filled situation.

Ask God to reveal why some circumstances foster impatience in you.

Patience is the companion of wisdom.
Saint Augustine of Hippo

THE GHOST OF SELFISHNESS PAST

Be generous, and you will be prosperous. Help others, and you will be helped.

Proverbs 11:25 GNT

In Charles Dickens' *A Christmas Carol*, Scrooge initially had one goal in life—to look out for Number One. His sole focus was to hold on to his riches and add to his wealth at every opportunity. Pursuing a single purpose seems to be one way to achieve a simple life. But Scrooge's miserly tendencies complicated his life by consuming his time, his energy, and his love. Only through generosity is Scrooge ultimately able to find joy and purpose and begin leading a simple, meaningful life.

Generosity makes your life simpler by giving you freedom. It frees you from striving to hold on to things you ultimately cannot keep, such as your time, money, and possessions. This freedom from striving further frees you to share the gifts God has given you with others, which, in turn, fosters relationships, community, and a more thankful heart. The more you give away, the more you recognize just how much God has given you to begin with.

True generosity is not determined by the size of a gift. Jesus praised a widow for giving away two small coins. Though her gift was tiny compared to the offerings of others, to her it was a great sacrifice.

Just like the widow, the gifts you give are not meant to be compared with the gifts of others. They are between you and God. You may be generous with your time by being a mentor or teacher. You may be generous with your wealth by writing a check to support a family halfway around the world. You may be generous with your possessions by practicing hospitality.

Whatever you give, true generosity goes beyond giving away what you have an overabundance of. It means taking an honest look at your lifestyle for any Scrooge-like tendencies and then giving beyond what is comfortable. This honest look will help release the hold selfishness has on your heart and free you to live a less self-centered and more God-centered life.

One Final Thought

The chains of selfishness cannot hold a heart that practices sacrificial giving.

Thoughts for Living Simply

Remember that the person who plants few seeds will have a small crop; the one who plants many seeds will have a large crop. You should each give, then, as you have decided, not with regret or out of a sense of duty; for God loves the one who gives gladly. And God is able to give you more than you need, so that you will always have all you need for yourselves and more than enough for every good cause.

2 Corinthians 9:6–8 GNT

A cheerful giver does not count the cost of what he gives. His heart is set on pleasing and cheering him to whom the gift is given.

Julian of Norwich

We must remember the words of the Lord Jesus. He said, "It is more blessed to give than to receive."

Acts 20:35 NIRV

As the purse is emptied, the heart is filled.

Victor Hugo

Remember...

_____Every gift you give away was originally a gift God gave to you.

_____God said that he loves cheerful givers.

_____Practicing generosity is one way of putting love into action.

_____Jesus was generous with his time, his words, and ultimately his life.

Simplify...

Practice generosity by practicing hospitality.

Give anonymously, whenever possible, because you will then be doing good without any expectation of reward.

Be generous with God's financial gifts.

Ask God to show you any Scrooge-like tendencies you may have that are complicating your life.

Schedule some time in your day so you can give it as a gift to someone who may need it.

We exist temporarily through what we take, but we live forever through what we give.
Douglas M. Lawson

THE IMPACT OF A LOVING LIFE

What we love we shall grow to resemble.
Saint Bernard of Clairvaux

The only thing that really counts is faith that shows itself
through love.
Galatians 5:6 NIRV

Let us love, not in word or speech, but in truth and action.
1 John 3:18 NRSV

This is what love is: it is not that we have loved God, but
that he loved us and sent his Son to be the means by which
our sins are forgiven. Dear friends, if this is how God loved
us, then we should love one another. No one has ever seen
God, but if we love one another, God lives in union with us,
and his love is made perfect in us.
1 John 4:10–12 GNT

You never can tell when you do an act
Just what the results will be
But with every deed you are sowing a seed,
Though the harvest you may not see.
Each kindly act is an acorn dropped
In God's productive soil;
You may not know, but the tree shall grow
With shelter for those who toil.
Ella Wheeler Wilcox

BUSY SIGNAL

*The most valuable of all talents is that of never using
two words when one will do.*

Thomas Jefferson

When Samuel Morse ushered in a new age of communication with the invention of the telegraph in the mid 1800s, the first message he sent asked an important question: "What hath God wrought?" Communication technology has come a long way. From high-speed Internet connections to cell phones with photo capabilities, you can almost reach anyone, anywhere, anytime. While God "hath wrought" human minds capable of inventing advanced telecommunications, the question you need to ask yourself is, "Do these tools really simplify my life?" While their purpose may be simplification, if you are not selective in how you use them, they may actually complicate your life.

Junk e-mail you didn't ask for demands your time to delete. Call waiting makes you weigh the importance of two different calls and put off one until later.

Cell phones ring at the most inopportune times. Or they don't ring at all, if you forget to recharge them. Every new communication's aid comes complete with an instruction manual you'll probably never have time to fully read, leaving you with a tool you'll never fully use.

Simplifying your life begins by recognizing that you do have a choice. You can turn off your cell phone when you're on vacation. You can let the answering machine pick up incoming calls while you're talking with your family around the dinner table. You can choose to pick up e-mail only once during the day.

You can choose the more efficient and effective methods of communication you have at your disposal. The Bible offers effective personal tools for communication. Biblical advice includes be brief, avoid long conversations that can be gossipy, communicate only when you have encouraging things to say, don't ramble, and don't pay attention to useless messages. Being selective in when, where, and how you communicate with others keeps your communication simple.

ONE FINAL THOUGHT

To simplify your communication, choose the most effective method and reject the least effective.

Thoughts for Living Simply

Remember that the person who plants few seeds will have Put away perversity from your mouth; keep corrupt talk far from your lips.
Proverbs 4:24 NIV

Try as hard as you like, but in the end only the language of the heart can ever reach another heart while mere words, as they slip from your tongue, don't get past your listener's ear.
Saint Francis de Sales

From the fruit of his mouth a man's stomach is filled; with the harvest from his lips he is satisfied.
Proverbs 18:20 NIV

Words, like eyeglasses, blur everything that they do not make clear.
Joseph Joubert

Remember...

_____Clear communication helps to avoid misunderstandings.

_____New technology does not always equal better communication.

_____You have several choices for communication, and the Bible gives ways to handle your communication with other people.

_____Communication becomes distraction when too many messages cloud your focus.

Simplify...

Consider getting caller ID or telemarketer blocker to keep communication with solicitors to a minimum.

Delete spam from your incoming e-mail immediately.

Turn off your cell phone and pager and let your answering machine pick up calls when you are having an in-depth conversation with someone.

Avoid long conversations on the phone about nothing.

Keep telephone calls and e-mail messages to a minimum while on vacation.

Banality is a symptom of non-communication.
Eugène Ionesco

DRINKING FROM THE WELL OF GOD'S PRESENCE

As a deer longs for a stream of cool water, so I long for you, O God. I thirst for you, the living God. When can I go and worship in your presence?

Psalm 42:1–2 GNT

The simple life is more easily attained when lived in concert with someone else. The presence of God is the fulfilling option to living alone. And daily time with God can help dispel discontentment, anxiety, even drivenness. Daily time with God can help you avoid spiritual dryness.

Spending time alone with God each day fills you with living water, which is like filling your water bottle before going on a long hike. Drinking a gallon of fluid before you leave and letting the bottle remain behind is unwise as well as uncomfortable. You need to take sips throughout your workout to keep your body well hydrated.

In the same way, filling your mind with God's Word and your heart with prayer each morning supplies you with something to sip on all day long. When you're stuck in traffic, a verse you read that morning may provide you with the ability to be patient. During a confrontation with a coworker, you might find yourself strangely at peace because you prayed about the situation earlier that day. You may even find yourself hearing God's voice more clearly throughout the day because you've spent time getting to know him better every morning.

The book of Psalms is filled with testimony of how drawing closer to God simplifies life. Among the benefits of spending time with God are peace, strength, comfort, power, and guidance. As the psalmist said, "I rely on your constant love; I will be glad, because you will rescue me. I will sing to you, O Lord because you have been good to me" (Psalm 13:5–6 GNT).

There are no set rules about entering God's presence other than to spend consistent time in prayer and Bible reading. You may want to write your own psalm, sing along with a gospel CD, memorize Scripture, or keep a journal about what God is teaching you. The key is to meet God with expectation, knowing that he alone is the refreshment and power you're truly thirsty for every day.

ONE FINAL THOUGHT

Your thirst for God is his gift to you to help draw you daily into the power of his presence.

Thoughts for Living Simply

Listen to my words, O Lord, and hear my sighs. Listen to my
cry for help, my God and king! I pray to you, O Lord; you hear
my voice in the morning; at sunrise I offer my prayer
and wait for your answer.
Psalm 5:1–3 GNT

*There is a God shaped vacuum in the heart of every man which cannot be
filled by any created thing, but only by God, the Creator,
made known through Jesus.*
Blaise Pascals

Jesus cried out, "Let anyone who is thirsty come to me, and let
the one who believes in me drink. As the scripture has said,
'Out of the believer's heart shall flow rivers of living water.'"
John 7:37–38 NRSV

My spirit has become dry because it forgets to feed on you.
Saint John of the Cross

Remember...

_____Time with God nourishes your spirit.

_____Jesus needed time in his father's presence to renew his spirit. Follow his example.

_____The presence of God can make even the most difficult day easier.

_____The more time you spend with God, the more you know how much you need him.

Simplify...

Schedule an appointment each day to meet with God and keep it.

Have a set place where you meet with God, and keep your study Bible, journal, pen, and headphones in this area.

Read a study Bible to help you better understand what God is saying.

Commit to memory a verse from your daily Bible reading to draw strength from during the day.

As a sponge is in the ocean and the ocean is in a sponge, so we are in God and God is in us.
Rufus Moseley

BLUEPRINT FOR A SIMPLER LIFE

God said to Noah, "This is how you are to build [the ark]"... Noah did everything just as God commanded him.

Genesis 6:15, 22 NIV

Building a house has a lot in common with building a life. You start with some raw materials, put in a lot of hard work, and hopefully end up with something that will stand the test of time. But no matter how high the quality of your materials or how intense your labor, chances are that if you don't start with a solid plan and seek godly advice, you'll end up with a mess instead of a house. The same is true for a purposeful life.

Reliance on God is key to a purposeful life as well as a surefire way to simplify everything that lies ahead of you. Planning saves you time, money, and frustration. Even God works his purposes in the world by a plan. When Adam and Eve chose to turn their backs on his original plan, God had a plan

130

for them to return to him. God promised to send a Savior who would pay for their sins and the sins of us who followed. He announced his plan through the words of the prophets hundreds of years before Christ was born. God developed a strategy and followed through to completion.

God's example—that of planning your steps before you move ahead—works when you are making plans of your own, regardless of the strategy you're trying to develop. It may be a plan for getting your finances under control, moving forward with your education, feeding your household for the week, or taking a vacation. Whatever your goal, ask God for wisdom first.

Next, write out a blueprint of what you want to accomplish, setting deadlines and listing specific action steps you need to take to reach your goal. Ask God to direct the design of your blueprint. As you move forward, check on your progress. Be flexible and make any changes needed. Then follow your plan through until the end. Recognize that God has the power to revise your plans along the way.

ONE FINAL THOUGHT

Making a plan with God's help before moving ahead makes the road to success an easier journey.

Thoughts for Living Simply

God declared, "I make known the end from the beginning,
from ancient times, what is still to come. I say: My purpose
will stand, and I will do all that I please . . . What I have said,
that will I bring about; what I have planned, that will I do."
Isaiah 46:10–11 NIV

*The value of life lies not in the length of days, but in the use we make
of them.*
Michel de Montaigne

You may make your plans, but God directs your actions.
Proverbs 16:9 GNT

*Planning is bringing the future into the present so you can do
something about it now.*
Alan Lakein

Remember...

_____Reliance on God is key to a purposeful life.

_____Starting with a solid plan and asking godly advice will help assure successful completion.

_____Planning saves you time, money, and frustration.

_____Seeking God's direction at the beginning of any project will point you in the right direction.

Simplify...

Write out practical steps you can take to reach your God-focused goals.

If a plan does not work out as you had hoped, retrace your steps to see where you may have failed to follow God's leading.

Help relieve financial stress before it happens by having a savings account for the unexpected.

Organize your time by penciling in deadlines for recurring tasks on your calendar.

Make sure you don't override God's inspiration.

In the power and splendor of the universe, inspiration waits for the millions to come.
John Masefield

WISE COUNSELORS

In an abundance of counselors there is safety.
Proverbs 11:14 NRSV

When a political leader takes public office, one of the first things on the agenda is to make sure he or she is surrounded by a group of trustworthy advisors. Surrounding oneself with advisors helps to simplify the complex job that lies ahead. After all, no one besides God is an expert on everything. Being able to turn to a group of people for advice, especially if those people are familiar with the leader's personal strengths and weaknesses, makes it easier for a politician to do the job.

But you don't have to lead a country to benefit from surrounding yourself with a group of people who support you. Placing yourself in the middle of a circle of friends and mentors is a simple way to help you be more successful in whatever job God has set before you.

Building a circle of support demands honesty—both with yourself and others. It takes humility, where people of different backgrounds, personalities, and opinions are willing to listen and learn from each other. It also takes time, and such relationships don't happen overnight. You must work with your colleagues and peers, pray with them, and share your heart with them. David relied on Ahithophel for advice: "In those days the advice Ahithophel gave was like that of one who inquires of God. That was how both David and Absalom regarded all of Ahithophel's advice" (2 Samuel 16:23 NIV).

Your best support group is found in your closest relationships. These relationships provide a mirror to help you see yourself more clearly. People who know you well and care about helping you reach your God-given potential are a great source of advice. They challenge you toward personal growth and away from mistakes that have the potential to complicate your life. They help you look your best, both inside and out.

One Final Thought

Surrounding yourself with a circle of honest, loving friends can give you the courage and support you need to achieve your potential.

Thoughts for Living Simply

Plans fail for lack of counsel, but with many advisers
they succeed.
Proverbs 15:22 NIV

Community is the place where God completes our lives with his joy.
Henri Nouwen

A wise man has great power, and a man of knowledge increases
strength; for waging war you need guidance, and for victory
many advisers.
Proverbs 24:5–6 NIV

*It is sometimes a point of as much cleverness to know to make good use
of advice from others as to be able give good advice to oneself.*
François, Duc de La Rochefoucauld

Remember...

_____Good advice can help simplify complex jobs.

_____The psalmist David, a man after God's heart, sought the wisdom of an advisor.

_____People who know you well are good sources of advice because they know you well.

_____Friendships are mirrors that help you see yourself more clearly.

Simplify...

Build a spiritual relationship with someone who can challenge, teach, and inspire you.

Ask your friends to help you see any blind spots you may have about your life and character.

Pray that you will make wise choices about who should be in your support group.

Strengthen the loving connection in your closest relationships by praying for those who support you.

Pray that your advisors will have the wisdom to guide you.

Sometimes our light goes out but is blown into flame by an encounter with another human being.
Albert Schweitzer

It's Wise to Downsize

*There is nothing so small but that we may honor God
by asking his guidance of it.*

John Ruskin

Downsizing your lifestyle is timely advice. The essence of downsizing is concentrating your focus and getting rid of things in your lifestyle that don't fit. Concentrating your focus simplifies your life by helping you target your efforts to what you've determined to be most important.

Jesus came to earth with a big goal—to save humanity—and he chose to concentrate the focus of his actions. His message was universal, yet he visited only one small corner of the world in person. His ability to heal disease and raise the dead could have occupied all of his time. For that matter, so could the opportunities he had for individual counseling, speaking engagements, or even fulfilling many of his followers' expectations by becoming a king.

The pull to do more must have tugged at Jesus' heart at

times. But Jesus made the most of his time by choosing to not take advantage of many opportunities. At times that meant turning his attention from teaching the crowds to hugging a small child. Jesus carefully chose to limit his lifestyle according to his father's wisdom and his ultimate goal.

But the pull to accomplish more is only one area you can evaluate when your goal is downsizing. Your lifestyle is more than your job. It's also the size of your home, the scope of your social life, the extent of your hobbies, your goals for retirement, and your expectations of a good life. Every area of your life has the potential to be downsized. Only God's wisdom and a clear, concentrated view of your true purpose in this life can help you know what to cut and what to throw your whole heart into.

ONE FINAL THOUGHT

Downsizing your life enlarges your impact by helping you focus more intently on what truly matters.

Thoughts for Living Simply

The Lord said, "They will be my people, and I will be their God. I will give them singleness of heart and action, so that they will always fear me for their own good."
Jeremiah 32:38–39 NIV

The sculptor produces the beautiful statue by chipping away such parts of the marble block as are not needed—it is a process of elimination.
Elbert Hubbard

Be wise enough not to wear yourself out trying to get rich.
Proverbs 23:4 GNT

One must be able to cut a knot, for everything cannot be untied; he must know how to disengage what is essential from the detail in which it is enwrapped, for everything cannot be equally considered; in a word, he must be able to simplify his duties, his business and his life.
Henri-Frédéric Amiel

Remember...

_____Jesus kept his main goal in mind, eliminating what didn't serve to reach that goal and then giving his whole heart to what remained.

_____The essence of down-sizing is concentration.

_____Doing a few things with excellence is better than doing a lot of things with mediocrity.

_____Small things are big things when they are the right things.

Simplify...

Write a purpose statement for yourself and honestly evaluate your activities to eliminate the ones that don't fit.

Critically evaluate each new opportunity to see if it fits your purpose statement.

Spend less time in the car by grouping weekly errands together and focus on running them all at one time.

If a new opportunity doesn't fit your purpose statement, don't do it.

Through excess the soul is made sick.
Saint Francis de Sales

THE GIFT OF A WELL-CHOSEN WORD

The genius of communication is the ability to be both totally honest and totally kind at the same time.
John Powell

A word fitly spoken is like apples of gold in a setting of sil-
ver. Like a gold ring or an ornament of gold is a wise rebuke
to a listening ear.
Proverbs 25:11–12 NRSV

May the words of my mouth and the meditation of my
heart be pleasing in your sight, O Lord, my Rock and my
Redeemer.
Psalm 19:14 NIV

May our Lord Jesus Christ himself and God our Father, who
loved us and by his grace gave us eternal encouragement and
hope, encourage your hearts and strengthen you in every
good deed and word.
2 Thessalonians 2:16–17 NIV

Conversation is but carving!
Give no more to every guest
Than he's able to digest.
Give him always of the prime,
And but little at a time.

Carve to all but just enough,
Let them neither starve nor stuff,
And that you may have your due,
Let your neighbor carve for you.

Jonathan Swift

FINDING YOUR STRIDE

We do not try to please people, but to please God, who tests our motives.
1 Thessalonians 2:4 GNT

Learning from the lives of others is one thing. Trying to be someone other than who God created you to be is quite another. Comparing yourself with others, and then trying to follow in their footsteps, can complicate your life.

Imagine what would happen if you were running a foot race. You're in the lead, but instead of keeping your eyes on the finish line, you keep looking over your shoulder. The person on the right is closing in. You evaluate her stride and decide to try to match it. It feels awkward and unnatural, but she obviously has some kind of advantage you're missing out on. Then you notice the guy on the left is wearing a pair of shorts that seem more aerodynamically suited to the current wind conditions. You veer off the track and head to the nearest department store to pick up a comparable set of running attire.

Sound ridiculous? It is. Yet trying to set the pace of your own life by imitating someone else will leave you in the dust just as surely as the decisions made in that imaginary foot race. God has a specific race planned just for you. It's a race being cheered on from heaven, but you're not running against anyone else. You're simply running toward Jesus. The Bible says that Jesus is the only one you are to follow.

Dare to be an original. Compare yourself with what God says you should be like, instead of with those around you, even those you admire. When you take your eyes off the finish line and focus on imitating others, it's easy to get off track. When you find your own stride, however, for the way God designed you, you fall into a more natural rhythm. So keep your eyes focused on Jesus. Then, put your heart into the race before you. That's the simplest and most direct way to come out ahead.

ONE FINAL THOUGHT

When you focus on running the race God has set before you,
you always come out a winner.

Thoughts for Living Simply

Be imitators of God, therefore, as dearly loved children and live a life of love, just as Christ loved us and gave himself up for us as a fragrant offering and sacrifice to God.
Ephesians 5:1–2 NIV

It is comparison that makes people miserable.
Ancient Proverb

Let us run with perseverance the race that is set before us, looking to Jesus the pioneer and perfecter of our faith, who for the sake of the joy that was set before him endured the cross, disregarding its shame, and has taken his seat at the right hand of the throne of God. Consider him who endured such hostility against himself from sinners, so that you may not grow weary or lose heart.
Hebrews 12:1–3 NRSV

Keeping up appearances is the most expensive thing in the world.
A. C. Benson

Remember...

_____The only thing God asks you to compare is your love to that of his Son.

_____Keeping your eyes on God makes it difficult to focus on comparing yourself to others.

_____God designed every individual as an original, never as a copy.

_____Comparing your life's story to another's is like comparing the book of John to that of Matthew—one can't be superior to the other, because each is unique.

Simplify...

Resist buying clothes or cars or electronic gadgets just because everybody else you know has them.

Pray regularly that God will prevent you from getting caught up in keeping up with the Joneses.

Develop a genuine interest in the unique race others are running.

Mute television commercials to avoid messages about a superficial life.

Look at every blessing as an incentive for praise, those you receive as well as those God gives to others.

God doesn't need me, but He desires me.
Steve Hawthorne

147

KEEPING YOUR HEAD IN THE CLOUDS

Our citizenship is in heaven.

Philippians 3:20 NIV

There is a home you've never been to, yet one your heart has longed for since birth. Heaven is your true home, your permanent address. Keeping your future destination in mind will help simplify your life here and now. It will help you sort your priorities by weighing what has eternal value against what does not. It will lighten your heart because you'll know that a home awaits you where there will be no more tears. It will also give you a realistic view of time. No one knows his or her moving date. Planning in light of that fact will encourage you to make the most of God's gift of today.

Planning to make a move to any new home in a distant country is a major undertaking. You have to pack light, choosing only what is truly essential. You talk to people who've visited your destination and read travel guides to help you prepare for what lies ahead. As your departure draws near, you purposefully set aside time to spend with those you'll be leaving behind. Everything you do is influenced in some way by your impeding move. The same should be true as you prepare for a future move to your eternal home in heaven.

Though firsthand accounts aren't available to help you prepare for your move, the Bible does provide a few travel tips. It says heaven is a real place and that Jesus is preparing a home there especially for you. It says treasures are already stored there for you, which means that any possessions here on earth will not be making the trip with you. The Bible also explains that all those who have a relationship with God will be making the move sooner or later.

Letting thoughts of heaven fill your mind can help you empty your life of what is unnecessary. At the same time it can draw you closer to the one you'll be spending eternity with. Anyway you look at it, taking time to contemplate heaven is an uplifting way to simplify your life.

ONE FINAL THOUGHT

Keeping heaven in mind helps you keep your life here on earth in line with God's perspective.

Thoughts for Living Simply

We know that when this tent we live in—our body here on earth—is torn down, God will have a house in heaven for us to live in, a home he himself has made, which will last forever.
2 Corinthians 5:1 GNT

He who has no vision of eternity will never get a true hold of time.
Thomas Carlyle

Jesus said, "Do not let your heart be troubled. Trust in God; trust also in me. In my Father's house are many rooms; if it were not so, I would have told you. I am going there to prepare a place for you. And if I go and prepare a place for you, I will come back and take you to be with me that you also may be where I am."
John 14:1–3 NIV

We talk about heaven being so far away. It is within speaking distance of those who belong there.
Dwight L. Moody

Remember...

_____Heaven is the home your heart truly longs for, but one which your mind cannot yet fully comprehend.

_____Today is just as much a part of eternity as your future in heaven.

_____When you cry, know that a day is coming when your tears will end.

_____The only perfect, simple life is the one awaiting you in heaven.

Simplify...

Find encouragement for today by talking with God about your future home.

Read Bible verses that talk about heaven to help you gain a clearer picture of what lies ahead.

When you find yourself trying to pack as many experiences into this life as possible, remember that you are going to live forever.

Weigh your priorities by asking yourself, "Will this make a difference in eternity?"

Jesus said, "The kingdom of heaven is like treasure hidden in a field."
Matthew 13:44 NIV

STEP BY STEP

Jesus said, "You shall be My witnesses both in Jerusalem, and in Judea and Samaria, and even to the remotest part of the earth."

Acts 1:8 NASB

Even the simplest of lives occasionally meets up with a complicated, gargantuan task. These tasks include one-time projects, such as preparing for a cross-country move, finishing your basement, or organizing a wedding. Or maybe you're faced with a time of medical rehabilitation or earning a college degree. Your hefty goal might even be relational, such as mending a rift with a family member. When first faced with a mission of this magnitude, you may feel overwhelmed, dwarfed by the immensity of what lies ahead.

But no matter how large your task, you can make it, and your life, simpler by breaking the project down into smaller, one-day-at-a-time-size responsibilities.

This "How do you eat an elephant? One bite at a time!" philosophy is demonstrated throughout the

Bible. Jesus' last words to his disciples were to go and share what he said with the rest of the world. Talk about an overwhelming task! But Jesus helped his followers see their ultimate goal in light of smaller victories.

First, they were to visit their own capital city, the people of Jerusalem. Next, they would venture into the adjoining regions of Judea and Samaria, reaching out to Gentiles as well as fellow Jews. By continuing to spread the good news this way, Jesus' followers would eventually reach the remotest parts of the earth. Their task was so big, it's still being tackled today by those who follow in the disciples' footsteps.

Tackling sizeable tasks in your own life can be made simpler by following this example. Know your ultimate goal. Break that goal down into a list of smaller tasks. Evaluate which tasks should be done first or which you have the time and resources to accomplish right now. Prioritize your remaining tasks, prayerfully evaluating your schedule and abilities. If you find your time or expertise lacking in any area, engage the help of others. Then go ahead and tackle that elephant—one bite at a time.

ONE FINAL THOUGHT

A mountain-size task is best conquered by following a determined path, one step at a time.

Thoughts for Living Simply

Jesus said, "I tell you the truth, if you have faith as small as a mustard seed, you can say to this mountain, 'Move from here to there' and it will move. Nothing will be impossible for you."
Matthew 17:20–21 NIV

Know what you want to do, hold the thought firmly, and do every day what should be done, and every sunset will see you that much nearer the goal.
Elbert Green Hubbard

The human mind plans the way, but the Lord
directs the steps.
Proverbs 16:9 NRSV

A pure, simple, and steadfast spirit is not distracted by the number of things to be done, because it performs them all to the honor of God, and endeavors to be at rest from self-seeking.
Thomas à Kempis

Remember...

_____God created the world by breaking his job down into a progression of separate miracles, such as the light, water, vegetation, animals, and people.

_____Jesus delegated some of the tasks to be accomplished to his disciples.

_____No matter how long it takes you to reach your goal, Jesus is beside you every step of the way.

_____Perseverance is as important as planning when it comes to tackling a long-term project.

Simplify...

Ask God for wisdom in breaking down large tasks, reducing your workload as well as your stress level.

Ask a close friend to help keep you accountable to meet the goals you set.

Schedule your most difficult tasks close to the beginning of a project to prevent procrastination.

Celebrate your progress periodically as you work toward your ultimate goal.

Praise God for every success along the way.

You never know how a horse will pull until you hook him to a heavy load.
Paul Bear Bryant

RETOOLING YOUR LIFE BY
TALKING WITH GOD

Prayer is the key of heaven; faith is the hand that turns it.
Thomas Watson

The world's most powerful vehicle for accomplishing your purpose is within your reach. By using prayer, coupled with exercise and discipline, you can become stronger, wiser, and more balanced in your approach to everyday life. It can expand your impact, as well as God's, on the world around you. At the same time, it offers you comfort in times of trouble and hope when you're on the verge of giving up. Most important, prayer is the key you need to build a relationship with the Creator of the universe—the only One who has the power to help you lead the simple life you long for, because prayer is about relationships more than about results.

Prayer simplifies your life, and God longs to not only hear requests, but also questions, confession, praise, and even complaints throughout your busy day. God is always within your reach, ready to respond with the power of both words and action.

Right before Jesus was arrested, he spent an intense time in prayer with his father. Jesus asked that he would not have to go through the suffering that he knew lay ahead. Then Jesus did something else. He expressed that what he wanted most was whatever his father knew would be best.

That is the true power of prayer. It changes more than circumstances. It changes hearts. The more time you spend talking to God, the more you get to know him better. The better you know him, the more you will trust God to answer your prayers in the way he knows is best. This is when you truly begin to live a simpler life. You will still have plenty of requests and concerns to bring to God, but you can rest in knowing that God is at work to answer your prayers.

Prayer is a multi-use tool that's always plugged into the ultimate source of power. You turn it on with simple conversation. There is no special posture or grammatical form to follow. It's fully operational once your heart is ready to humbly wield it.

ONE FINAL THOUGHT

Prayer is a powerful, multipurpose tool that can make a positive difference in any area of your life that you are trying to simplify.

Thoughts for Living Simply

The prayer of a godly person is powerful. It makes things happen.
James 5:16 NirV

Prayer is not merely expressing our present desires. Its purpose is to exercise and train our desires, so that we want what he is getting ready to give us. His gift is very great, and we are small vessels for receiving it. So prayer involves widening our hearts to God.
Saint Augustine of Hippo

Do not be anxious about anything, but in everything, by prayer and petition, with thanksgiving, present your requests to God. And the peace of God, which transcends all understanding, will guard your hearts and your minds in Christ Jesus.
Philippians 4:6–7 NIV

Certain thoughts are prayers. There are moments when, whatever be the attitude of the body, the soul is on its knees.
Victor Hugo

Remember...

_____Prayer is a two-way conversation—there's a time to speak and a time to listen for God's reply.

_____Getting in the habit of conversing with God through-out the day, even briefly, will help you better hear and understand his voice.

_____Prayer changes things, including your own heart.

_____Even a single word can be a heartfelt prayer.

Simplify...

If a friend shares a concern with you online, pray before you shut down your computer.

Actively look for answers to prayer with the awareness that God's answers may differ from what you expect.

Talk to God during your com-mute or as you do household chores.

Talk to God about any concern that is important enough for you to share with others.

Prayer is more than an order of words, the conscious occupation of the praying mind, or the sound of the voice praying.
T. S. Eliot

THE GRACIOUS GIFT OF CONVERSATION

Gold there is, and rubies in abundance, but lips that speak
knowledge are a rare jewel.

Proverbs 20:15 NIV

Every word you speak is a gift. The right word at the right time can provide the advice that helps turn someone's life around. It can comfort a mourning heart or give a friend the courage to try again. It can solve problems, organize schedules, or worship God. Carefully chosen words can help your life run more smoothly.

Watching your words—both good words and bad—is a positive step toward a simpler life. Desiring to let love motivate your conversation, listening carefully before you reply, and even holding your tongue altogether can all be ways of using your tongue to build understanding and deepen relationships, preventing problems before they have a chance to start.

The Bible compares your tongue with a bit that is used

to control a horse, or a rudder that controls the direction of a large ship. In other words, it may be small, but your tongue helps determine the direction in which you're going to move. If you choose to move ahead in the direction of simplicity, you need to make a conscious decision to give good verbal gifts. As you become more aware of what is coming out of your mouth, you'll develop more wisdom and control in knowing when to speak and when to remain silent.

Becoming more aware of your words begins with prayer. Ask God to help you think before you speak and nudge you toward words that build others up. Read the book of Proverbs, which is filled with useful advice, such as "Listen before you answer" (18:13 GNT) and "Stay away from people who talk too much" (20:19 GNT). Asking a good friend to be a sounding board and give you feedback on how well you're communicating is another practical way of watching your words. The more control you have over your tongue, the better gifts you'll be able to give, and the simpler your life will be.

ONE FINAL THOUGHT

Every word you're about to give away is worth weighing before it's spoken.

161

Thoughts for Living Simply

All of us often make mistakes. But if a person never makes a mistake in what he says, he is perfect and is also able to control his whole being. We put a bit into the mouth of a horse to make it obey us. And we are able to make it go where we want. Or think of a ship: big as it is and driven by such strong winds, it can be steered by a very small rudder, and it goes wherever the pilot wants it to go. So it is with the tongue: small as it is, it can boast about great things.

James 3:2–5 GNT

Silence, along with modesty, is a great aid to conversation.

Michel De Montaigne

Let your speech always be with grace, as though seasoned with salt, so that you will know how you should respond to each person.

Colossians 4:6 NASB

Let our conversation now be without precedent in fact or literature, each one speaking to the best of his ability the truth to the best of his knowledge.

Samuel Beckett

Remember...

_____When God gives the gift of his perfect words, they always fit just right.

_____Your words can be just what someone in your life needs to hear today.

_____Jesus used words to open the minds and heal the hearts and bodies of those around him.

_____The perfect gift, including the gift of words, comes at the right time, wrapped in the right way, offered to just the right person.

Simplify...

Give words of encouragement and praise freely.

Use your words wisely, lovingly, and sparingly during tense situations.

Say "Can we discuss this further later? I'd like to think about what you said before replying" if you find yourself at a loss for how to reply in a positive way.

Apologize promptly anytime you realize that you have spoken inappropriately.

Stop gossip before it starts by only discussing problems with those directly involved in the situation.

Words, how potent for good and evil in the hands of one who knows how to use them.
Nathaniel Hawthorne

The Effectiveness of a Focused Heart

God requires a faithful fulfillment of the merest trifle given us to do, rather than the most ardent aspiration to things to which we are not called.

Saint Francis de Sales

Serve wholeheartedly, as if you were serving the Lord, not men, because you know that the Lord will reward everyone for whatever good he does.

Ephesians 6:7–8 NIV

Teach me, Lord, what you want me to do, and I will obey you faithfully; teach me to serve you with complete devotion.

Psalm 86:11 GNT

Whatever your task, put yourselves into it, as done for the Lord and not for your masters, since you know that from the Lord you will receive an inheritance as your reward; you serve the Lord Christ.

Colossians 3:23–24 NRSV

All that you do,
Do with your might;
Things done in halves
Are never done right.

One thing each time,
And that done well,
Is a very good rule,
As many can tell.

Moments are useless
Trifled away;
So work while you work,
And play while you play.

M. A. Stodart

BECOMING A BIG PICTURE PERSON

Be joyful always; pray continually; give thanks in all circumstances,
for this is God's will for you in Christ Jesus.

1 Thessalonians 5:16–18 NIV

The more you get to know God, the more natural it will be to see things from his perspective. When you take what you see and balance it against what you know about God—his love for you and others, his holiness, his mercy, and his plans for eternity—your options become clearer, making it easier to determine the right course of action to take in any situation.

You see the world through human eyes. Whether you wear contacts, glasses, or have 20/20 vision, what you see communicates a message to you. But it takes more than your eyes to understand what you're seeing. When you see a mountain in the distance, it looks as though it's small enough to hold in your hand. What you know about mountains and about human sight, however, will affect how

166

you interpret what you see as well as the actions you decide to take based on that interpretation. The more accurate your interpretation, the wiser and more effective your subsequent actions will be.

Gaining the proper perspective—God's perspective—simplifies your life. Seeing the Big Picture behind everyday situations helps you differentiate between a big deal and a small one, find opportunities hidden within inconveniences, even experience joy in the middle of difficulty. It allows you to see a job you once thought tedious—raking leaves, for instance—as a chance to enjoy God's beauty of the changing seasons. It can turn the harsh words uttered by a boss into an opportunity to see how deeply he is hurting after a recent divorce and exercise compassion.

The truest perspective available comes from only one source—God. Learning to see the world through God's eyes is like looking through a telescope. You realize there is so much more going on than what can be seen with the human eye.

ONE FINAL THOUGHT

It is easier to make a sound decision when you are able to see a situation from a heavenly perspective.

Thoughts for Living Simply

We do not lose heart. Though outwardly we are wasting away, yet inwardly we are being renewed day by day. For our light and momentary troubles are achieving for us an eternal glory that far outweighs them all. So we fix our eyes not on what is seen, but on what is unseen. For what is seen is temporary, but what is unseen is eternal.
2 Corinthians 4:16–18 NIV

To see a world in a grain of sand and a heaven in a wild flower: Hold infinity in the palm of your hand, and eternity in an hour.
William Blake

We know that God causes all things to work together for good to those who love God, to those who are called according to His purpose.
Romans 8:28 NASB

An adventure is only an inconvenience rightly considered.
G. K. Chesterton

Remember...

_____You can often see the good God promises to work in every situation by looking through his eyes.

_____In God's eyes, you are perfect.

_____Jesus willingly chose to go to the cross because he chose to see things from his father's eternal perspective.

_____The more you see life through God's eyes, the more joy you'll find in your heart.

Simplify...

Weigh your emotions against what God says about a difficult situation before taking action.

Resolve to see your difficulties from God's perspective.

Learn to recognize when your attitude needs adjusting, then take the time to regain a proper perspective.

Look for something positive in every seemingly negative situation and thank God for it.

Schedule a mini-retreat to talk to God about your spiritual big picture.

It's very hard to take yourself too seriously when you look at the world from outer space.
Thomas K. Mattingly II

CALM, COOL, AND SPIRITUALLY COLLECTED

Take from our souls the strain and stress, and let our
ordered lives confess, the beauty of thy peace.

John Greenleaf Whittier

Stress gets a lot of bad publicity. High blood pressure, indigestion, insomnia, lack of ability to concentrate, and irritability are just a few of the problems often attributed to it. But stress plays a positive part in even the simplest of lifestyles. Stress triggers that surge of adrenaline that communicates "Brake now!" to your body when another car almost merges into your front bumper. Stress is a natural and necessary part of daily life. The problem occurs when you are under stress so frequently that your body forgets how to calm down, even after the source of stress is gone.

Learning to use stress to stimulate action when needed, and then to turn off your body's response afterward, is a necessary safeguard for the simple life. To do this, you need to be aware of what your own personal stressors are.

Consider what normal situations make your adrenaline surge. If any of your habits contribute to increasing stress levels in your life, ask God to help you deal with them in a positive, productive way. Control what you can control.

If you know a stressful situation lies ahead, prepare yourself. The night before Jesus went to the cross, he was obviously under incredible stress. What did he do? He went off by himself to spend time with his heavenly father. Retreat to a quiet spot. Focus on God and cast your cares on him.

Sometimes, stress arises without warning. In these cases, take a break when you feel your blood pressure rising. Treat yourself to your favorite form of relaxation. Talk to God. Take a walk. Laugh with a friend. Read a book. Sing along with a Christian CD. Play a round of golf. Relax in the tub. Before, during, or after stressful situations, a few moments of physical and spiritual relaxation can keep stress from having a negative effect on your life.

ONE FINAL THOUGHT

Relieving your body of unwanted stress is good for your physical and spiritual health.

Thoughts for Living Simply

Jesus said, "Come to me, all you that are weary and are carrying heavy burdens, and I will give you rest. Take my yoke upon you, and learn from me; for I am gentle and humble in heart, and you will find rest for your souls. For my yoke is easy, and my burden is light."
Matthew 11:28–30 NRSV

The beginning of anxiety is the end of faith. The beginning of true faith is the end of anxiety.
George Mueller

Cast your cares on the Lord and he will sustain you; he will never let the righteous fall.
Psalm 55:22 NIV

Worry can rob you of happiness, but kind words will cheer you up.
Proverbs 12:25 GNT

Remember...

_____It is not stress itself, but what you do with stress, that determines whether it is harmful or beneficial.

_____The night before Jesus went to the cross he was under stress, and he went off by himself to spend time with his heavenly father.

_____God's peace is always available for the asking—regardless of external circumstances.

_____Getting rid of today's stress leaves your body better able to handle any stress that may arise tomorrow.

Simplify...

Make a list of what relaxes you—prayer, contemplation, Bible reading—and try one of the ideas whenever you're feeling stressed.

Watch a movie that makes you laugh to help release physical tension.

Sing in the car, dance to the stereo, or walk around the block after a stressful day.

Control what you can control and don't stress over what you can't.

Determine which of your habits contribute to stress—perhaps procrastination or disorganization—and ask God to help you deal with them in a positive way.

You will break the bow if you keep it always bent.
Greek Proverb

SIMPLE WAYS TO HONOR SPECIAL DAYS

The soul of one who loves God always swims in joy, always keeps holiday, and is always in the mood for singing.

Saint John of the Cross

Think Christmas, Easter, Mother's Day, weddings, and birthday celebrations. What do those words bring to your mind? If the thought of Christmas, or any other holiday or celebration, unleashes an endless to-do list in your mind, it's time to simplify.

How life's special days are celebrated are as diverse as the people celebrating them. Some celebrations are simple, while others rival a regal coronation. If simplifying your life is your goal, simplifying your celebrations is one way of helping you accomplish your goal. After all, when it comes to celebrating, there are no hard and fast rules. Success can truly only be measured by the heart.

Jesus performed his first miracle by helping make a wedding celebration a success. Back in Jesus' day, wedding receptions lasted for days. Running out of food or wine during the extended celebration reflected very poorly on the newlyweds and their parents. So when Jesus found out that the wine supply was running low before the party was over, he miraculously, yet quietly, turned mere water into wine. Jesus' loving actions enhanced the celebration, because he kept his focus on what really mattered—honoring the bride and groom and their families.

Simplifying your own celebrations begins with finding that same focus. Ask yourself, "What am I celebrating? Whom am I trying to honor? What is the best way to get that message across?" While traditions are an important form of celebration and remembrance, they are only as useful as they are pleasurable for you, as well as your guests.

Before you plan "the usual" for any kind of celebration, reevaluate your time, budget, and traditions. Creatively brainstorm ways to simplify, replace, or eliminate traditions that overwhelm your time and energy. Then, join in the joy of celebrating with a lighter and more carefree heart.

ONE FINAL THOUGHT

Focusing on the purpose of a celebration adds to the festivity as well as helps promote the simplicity of any event.

Thoughts for Living Simply

One generation will commend your works to another; they will tell of your mighty acts . . . They will celebrate your abundant goodness and joyfully sing of your righteousness.
Psalm 145:4, 7 NIV

All life is a celebration for us; we are convinced, in fact, that God is always everywhere. We sing while at work, we sing hymns while we sail, we pray while we carry on life's other occupations.
Clement of Alexandria

This is a day you are to commemorate; for the generations to come you shall celebrate it as a festival to the Lord—a lasting ordinance.
Exodus 12:14 NIV

The art of being happy lies in the power of extracting happiness from common things.
Henry Ward Beecher

Remember...

_____God should be at the center of everything worth celebrating.

_____Celebrations don't have to unleash an endless to-do list.

_____Celebrations can be as diverse as the people celebrating them.

_____Traditions are only as useful as they are pleasurable for the people celebrating them.

Simplify...

Make a card file of those you regularly give gifts to, listing their favorite hobbies, interests, and colors to spark unique gift ideas.

Keep a stack of birthday, anniversary, congratulations, and sympathy cards on hand.

Stick a candle in a large cookie, or even the dinner entrée, if the thought of baking a cake stresses you out.

Reevaluate your time, budget, and traditions each time you plan a celebration.

If we do not find God in the duties and relationships of the common day, it is not likely we shall find him at all.
James S. Stewart

LET THE SPARKS FLY

Jesus said, "If you forgive others the wrongs they have done to you, your Father in heaven will also forgive you."

Matthew 6:14 GNT

Throughout your lifetime, you'll find relationships at the heart of your deepest joys. While some relationships add to your laughter and help dry your tears, others may leave you feeling wounded and weary. It seems that one logical way to simplify your life would be to cut off complicated relationships. But God has another idea.

God cares a lot about healing relationships, even difficult ones. That's why Jesus came to earth. God's example of humility, forgiveness, and unconditional love is the perfect one to follow when you're faced with reconciling a troubled relationship. God took the initiative to reach out to those who had turned their backs on him. You can emulate that action by being the first to move toward reconciliation, regardless of who is at fault.

178

Hands that reach out in reconciliation freely offer forgiveness. Forgiving others, especially those who refuse to reconcile or acknowledge their own part in a problem, is downright difficult. The key is remembering how much God has forgiven you—then extending that same grace to others. Even after you've forgiven someone, angry feelings may still arise. You may need to exercise your choice to forgive again.

At the heart of forgiveness is unconditional love. Only God can offer that gift perfectly. However, God has provided you with a practical classroom for learning how to love without reservation. The doors of that classroom opened the moment God placed people of different temperaments together on earth. By working together, living together, and learning to love each other, people's lives compliment as well as challenge one other. The Bible compares this process to "iron sharpening iron."

But you can learn by doing. Forgiving is God's answer to simplifying your relational life. Following his example will help you replace hurt with healing and harmony. That's a lesson worth studying, applying, and benefiting from.

ONE FINAL THOUGHT

Reconciliation helps untangle your troubles through lessons in love.

Thoughts for Living Simply

Bear with each other and forgive whatever grievances you may have against one another. Forgive as the Lord forgave you. And over all these virtues put on love, which binds them all together in perfect unity.
Colossians 3:13–14 NIV

The only true forgiveness is that which is offered and extended even before the offender has apologized and sought it.
Sören Kierkegaard

If it is possible, as far as it depends on you, live at peace with everyone.
Romans 12:18 NIV

Search thy own heart; what paineth thee in others in thyself may be.
John Greenleaf Whittier

Remember...

_____Forgiveness is a gift.

_____The person you consider difficult may be just the tool God has decided you need to sharpen dull areas of your   own life.

_____Jesus knew a relationship with you would be a difficult one, yet he risked building   one with you anyway.

_____Being quick to listen, slow to speak, and slow to become angry is a positive way to handle each and every relationship.

Simplify...

Write out what you are going to say before trying to reconcile a difficult relationship.

Deal with any relational problems as soon as they arise.

Keep your relationship with God tangle-free by daily confessing anything you have done that goes against God's law of loving.

When discussing emotional topics, repeat in your own words what the other person is saying.

Ask God for wisdom in determining whether to confront a relational situation, overlook an offense, or ask for forgiveness.

Everyone should keep a fair-sized cemetery in which to bury the faults of others.
Henry Ward Beecher

It All Comes Down to One Thing

You, Lord, give perfect peace to those who keep their purpose firm
and put their trust in you.

Isaiah 26:3 GNT

One of the most significant steps you can make toward
leading a simple life is acknowledging one simple
truth—God is God, and you are not. This may
sound simplistic, but trusting God with all you
have, all you are, and all you'd love to do in
this life is a choice you have to make each and
every day.

Trusting God lets you put faith into action.
It's like a child faced with taking the training
wheels off of her first two-wheeler. Looking
at the instability of the bike and knowing
her own lack of experience makes the task
daunting. But encouraged by the gentle push
of a loving parent who promises not to let her
fall, she is able to conquer her fears and move
forward in faith.

Taking off the training wheels of your
own resources and abilities means trusting

God enough to let him lead you in new directions. To do this, you need to act on what God asks you to do, whether through the Bible or personally in prayer. Acting on what God asks you to do will help you mature in areas such as loving others unconditionally, giving generously, working diligently, praying consistently, and handling what God has given you responsibly.

Just like riding a bike feels increasingly more effortless as time goes by, so will trusting God. As you continue to take God at his word and find him faithful, your grip on what is unnecessary will begin to loosen, further simplifying your life. Your wholehearted, childlike trust will help you let go of possessions that hold an empty promise of contentment.

God knows the journey that lies ahead of you. He wants you to experience the joy and freedom that is found in trusting him with every detail of your life. Putting your abilities, fears, cares, and future into his hands releases you to live the eternal adventure of a full, yet simple, life

ONE FINAL THOUGHT

The essence of the simple life is trusting God to help you make the most of each and every day in a way that honors him.

Thoughts for Living Simply

Trust in the Lord and do good; live in the land and be safe.
Seek your happiness in the Lord and he will give you your
heart's desire. Give yourself to the Lord; trust in him, and he
will help you; he will make your righteousness shine like the
noonday sun.
Psalm 37:3–6 GNT

Faith strips the mask from the world and reveals God in everything. It
makes nothing impossible and renders meaningless such words as anxiety,
danger, and fear so that the believer goes through life calmly and peace-
fully, with profound joy—like a child, hand-in-hand with his mother.
Charles de Foucauld

If it is possible, as far as it depends on you, live at peace with
everyone.
Romans 12:18 NIV

Whatever happens, abide steadfast in a determination to cling
simply to God.
Saint Francis de Sales

Remember...

_____Living a simple life means trusting God's love every step of the way.

_____The more something, or someone, is tested and found to hold true, the easier it is to extend your wholehearted trust.

_____Jesus trusted his Father's plan for his life on earth, even when it looked impossible.

_____There is no better, simpler plan for your life than the one God has for you.

Simplify...

Build your trust in God by reading the Bible and watching God work in your life.

Take each and every worry to God and leave them with him in prayer.

Keep God's priorities of loving him and others in mind when trying to simplify any area of your life.

Ask others whose faith seems stronger than your own why they trust in God.

Admit to God any areas you have trouble trusting him in—ask for his help to make your faith grow.

The believer has leaned forward, heard the whisper, and trusted it to be the voice of God.
Fred Craddock

THE FREEDOM OF FAITH

Purity of heart and simplicity are of great force with almighty God, who is in purity most singular, and of nature most simple.
Gregory the Great

Faith is being sure of what we hope for. It is being certain of what we do not see. That is what the people of long ago were praised for. We have faith. So we understand that everything was made when God commanded it. That's why we believe that what we see was not made out of what could be seen.
Hebrews 11:1–3 NIRV

Jesus said, "If you hold to my teaching, you are really my disciples. Then you will know the truth, and the truth will set you free."
John 8:31–32 NIV

We walk by faith, not by sight.
2 Corinthians 5:7 NRSV

"Keep this for me."
What child has not said this,
And placed a treasure in his mother's hand
With strict injunction she should keep it safe
Till he return?
He knows with her it will be safe;
No troubled thought or anxious fear besets his mind,
And off he runs lighthearted to his play.

If children can so trust, why cannot we,
And place our treasures, too, in God's safe hand;
Our hopes, ambitions, needs, and those we love,
Just see them, in his all embracing care,
And say with joyous heart, "They are with Thee."

Author Unknown

*Better to eat a dry crust with peace
of mind than have a banquet in a
house full of trouble.*
Proverbs 17:1 GNT

Godliness is actually a means of great gain when accompanied by contentment. For we brought nothing into the world, so we cannot take anythout out of it either. If we have food and covering, with these we shall be content.

1 Timothy 6:6–8 NASB

God is able to make all grace abound to you, so that in all things at all times, having all that you need, you will abound in every good work.

2 Corinthians 9:8 NIV